PROSPER!

How to Prepare for the Future and Create a World Worth Inheriting

CHRIS MARTENSON, PhD & ADAM TAGGART

MORE INFORMATION YOU CAN'T AFFORD TO LIVE WITHOUT

PROSPER!

How to Prepare for the Future and Create a World Worth Inheriting

CHRIS MARTENSON, PhD
& ADAM TAGGART

Peak Prosperity Books is an imprint of RDA Press, LLC
RDA Press, LLC.
15170 N. Hayden Road
Scottsdale, AZ 85260

Printed in the United States of America

First Edition: 2015 ISBN: 978-1-937832-76-6

CONTENTS

FOREWORD
BY ROBERT KIYOSAKI

THE PRICE OF BAD ADVICE

In 1970, if someone put $1 million in the bank, they might have received $150,000 in annual interest. In 1970, you could live on $150,000 a year.

In 2015, if someone puts $1 million in the bank, they might receive $10,000 a year in interest. If that family attempts to live on $10,000 a year, they are technically below the poverty line, although—technically—"millionaires."

And yet financial experts continue to say, "Save money." Why would anyone save money when banks and governments are printing money?

But wait, it gets worse.

Financial advisors recommend people "Invest for the long term." Yet after 2007, HFT, high frequency trading, began dominating the market. While mom and pop are "investing for the long term," HFT traders are trading in milliseconds and microseconds.

So who made the most money after China devalued their currency and global stock markets crashed? I'll give you a hint: It was not the mom-and-pop long-term investors.

People investing for the long term in the stock market are like savers—the next big losers.

In 2002, *Rich Dad's Prophecy* was published. *Prophecy* predicted that the biggest stock market crash in history was coming in 2016. *Prophecy* also predicted an initial major crash that would arrive prior to the giant crash of 2016. That initial crash arrived in October 2007, when the Dow headed south and the subprime crisis took Lehman Brothers and other down.

My point is, this collapse was predictable to those who were paying attention. In my 60-minute video titled, *The Man Who Could See The Future*, offered for free from The Rich Dad Company, you can see footage of me on national television prior to October, warning people of the coming crash and downfall of Lehman Brothers.

My prediction of an even larger market crash in 2016—one that will result in tremendous wealth destruction for many—still stands. Again, those paying attention are seeing signs of instability everywhere.

But this time, the threat is not just economic. Critical systems and global resources we depend on for our modern way of life are starting to fail. There will be few places to take shelter from this coming storm.

Following bad advice at a time like this is not just risky. It's dangerous.

THE VALUE OF GOOD ADVICE

The year 2016 is just around the corner. We all need to prepare for what's coming, and there's little time left. That is why I am endorsing *Prosper!* I know Chris and Adam well—these guys have more than a crystal ball.

They have an actionable framework for building true wealth (it's about more than simply money) and combine it with sound advice for how to face the tremendous challenges that lie dead ahead. They lay out specific steps that will not only make you much less vulnerable to the coming disruption, but will position you to prosper greatly when it arrives. I've already put many of these steps into practice in my own life.

I loved Chris' first book, *The Crash Course*, and I love *Prosper!*

Those who are well positioned when crisis hits make fortunes overnight. Unfortunately, those following bad advice (like that offered by most financial advisors today) are wiped out.

I want you to prosper in the years ahead. The coming crash of 2016 may be your biggest opportunity to do so if you prepare wisely in advance. And that's why I encourage you to read *Prosper!* today, not tomorrow.

– Robert Kiyosaki

ACKNOWLEDGMENTS

Creating a book requires a substantial sacrifice of time and energy from many other people than just its authors. This book is no exception.

While the list of those who helped make this book possible is long, several people deserve special recognition:

Garrett Sutton and Mona Gambetta for their championship and tireless efforts in mobilizing the team at RDA Press to publish this work under an ambitiously tight time schedule.

Ken Harp, Susan Kammerzell, Jason Wiskerchen and Becca Martenson for their service as chapter reviewers and their excellent feedback, which were invaluable additions to the authors' best efforts.

Ron and Peg Stewart for generously providing the remote cabin retreat where the planning and concept work for this book was carried out.

Maryann Taggart for designing the visuals that appear throughout the chapters.

Kenny McElroy, because many of the ideas in here were jarred loose that day on the back trails of Sedona, along with a few molars.

The thousands of participants in our Peak Prosperity seminars, but especially the few hundreds that have attended the intimate gatherings at the Rowe Conference Center, who helped us shape and refine the material in this book over the years.

The millions of wonderful, dedicated visitors to the PeakProsperity.com website for inspiring and encouraging us to share this message of resilience more widely, and who were patient with us as we hunkered down to write this book.

Finally and most importantly: our wives and children for their tolerance and support during the long months we were absorbed with writing, being generally negligent as husbands and fathers. For Chris, that's Becca, Erica, Simon and Grace. For Adam, it's Ashley, Merritt and Charlotte. To us, you are the most valuable form of capital.

With great gratitude,
Chris & Adam

INTRODUCTION

You can feel it in your bones: the world is in crisis. You see the signs every day. They are in the overabundance of depressing news, revealed by overly-stressed natural systems, and telegraphed by the emotional strains exhibited by people you know.

This gathering of warning signs is likely the reason you picked up this book.

But what you may not yet know is that this state of crisis is going to intensify over the next several decades—possibly to a breaking point.

Why?

Because we're living in an age of dangerous imbalances. There's too much debt in the world and too little economic growth to service it. There are too few fish in the ocean and there is way too much carbon dioxide in the atmosphere. There are too many paper claims on the world's wealth and far too few tangible resources backing those claims.

A global population of 7.2 billion here in 2015 is projected to expand to 9 or even 10 billion by 2050, requiring vast additional amounts of food, fresh water, and mineral resources. At some point within the next ten years, global oil supplies will very likely peak, which means the cheap energy that has propelled the global economy over the past 100 years will be gone forever.

For every one calorie of food you eat, *ten* calories of (rapidly depleting) fossil fuels are stealthily expended in producing it. The majority of the nutrients in the world's agricultural soils have been so horribly degraded by industrial farming practices, that our farmlands now *need* a continuous supply of chemical fertilizers just so plants can still grow. But these modern fertilizers are made from depleting fossil fuels, creating the obvious long-term predicament: *How will we grow more food for more people with less energy?*

We can ask the same question about the future of the global economy, as it depends on these same depleting fossil fuels for its growth. And yet, financial markets are currently priced as if nothing is wrong and never will be.

We humans keep simply consuming more and more without limit (while calling it a 'healthy economy').

Knowing this, you can detect the obvious contradiction that practically nobody talks about in public: our modern lifestyle has become a system of extraction that always requires *more of everything* but we live on a finite planet. Quite literally, this means our entire way of life is unsustainable. By definition, anything that is unsustainable will someday end. Because of the way our various complex support systems are configured, we have to face the idea that we do not just risk a future of hardship, but the prospect of *collapse*.

So you feel it in your bones that something big is about to shift and that the status quo simply can't continue for much longer. Perhaps you just *know* that there are things you need to be doing, *right now*, to get ready. But you don't know exactly what's coming, when it will arrive, or how big the disruption will be. It might be another deep economic recession. Or a global military conflict. Or an energy crisis. Or perhaps the rains will stop falling on our most important farmlands while falling too heavily elsewhere. It may be any or all of these things, or something entirely different that kicks off a long era of disruptive adjustments.

How all of this turns out is anybody's guess, but the biggest *losing* bet anyone could make would be in assuming that everything will simply continue on smoothly, more or less as they have in the past. Given the warning signs it's obvious that the next 20 years are going to be completely unlike the last 20 years.

But this doesn't need to mean a lifetime of calamity for you. Not if you take prudent action today.

But what actions should you take exactly? And in which order and will anything you do really make any difference?

The answer to that last question is a resounding 'Yes!'. At our website PeakProsperity.com, years of collecting and sharing insights with millions of people who are preparing for these changes have yielded a treasure trove of specific activities and examples. Compiling them into a digestible action plan is the reason we wrote this book.

Taking the right steps now will give you the critical advantage of *Resilience*. Resilience is the ability to recover quickly from adversity, and will be the key to not merely persevering through the coming era of change, but to thriving within it.

This book will instruct you on how to become more resilient and engaged in ways that will guarantee a better outcome for you and your loved ones *no matter which future arrives*. If the predicted crises arrive, you'll be positioned to sail through them better than 99% of the rest of the population. And if they don't materialize, you'll still be much better off than you are today.

So whether you want to protect against risk, or simply just live better, this book is your invitation to:

- Become healthier
- Be more financially secure
- Have deeper and more fulfilling relationships
- Live a life of purpose
- Be happier
- Surround yourself with abundance and beauty

Seriously, who *wouldn't* want these benefits?

These aren't the idle hopes of a few starry-eyed dreamers. They're the actual outcomes we've achieved in our own lives, as have thousands of PeakProsperity.com community members, after first detecting the approaching storm clouds and then taking the specific actions outlined in this book with a sense of purpose and optimism. But don't just take our word for it. Read the many stories of personal growth woven throughout the coming chapters and judge for yourself.

Our mission is to create a world worth inheriting. After a decade of research, implementation, and evangelization, we've realized the path boils down to this truism: *You have to become the change you wish to see in the world.*

It's at once both that simple and that hard.

'Simple' because changing ourselves is the one thing that's 100% within our control.

'Hard' because change takes effort, and takes us out of our comfort zones. It often means going against the herd, which takes discipline, courage, and a thick skin. Most people will wait until the last minute once the crisis has arrived, which is far too late to properly prepare.

For example, during the writing of this book in early summer 2015, the panicked people of Greece started lining up at ATMs to withdraw their money only *after* the country's banking system had shut down. The mass's magical thinking that "Everything will somehow work out" left them flat-footed when things didn't work out. In contrast, prudent minds that had been paying attention removed their funds much earlier, having heeded the parade of warning signs over the prior few years.

The vast majority of people out there, just like the good citizens of Greece, will wait until a crisis strikes before allowing the reality of present circumstances to penetrate their mental defenses. It's simply how humans are wired.

This is why a good portion of this book is dedicated not just to physical action, but to the emotional and psychological preparation necessary to persevere and even thrive amidst turbulent times.

If you've read this far, we can already tell you're the kind of person uncomfortable leaving the future up to fate alone. If you're ready to start shaping your destiny, this book is for you.

Resilience is not something you acquire and are done with; it's a life-long process of refinement and improvement. Done the right way, becoming resilient is incredibly worthwhile and rewarding. And if you set out on this path, we guarantee you'll be vastly more prepared and prosperous in the coming decades than those who ignore the signs of coming change.

Preparing for this new future, whatever it ultimately may be, is simultaneously the greatest challenge and opportunity of our lifetimes. We say this as fellow pilgrims on the journey who happen to have gotten started a few years ago and can therefore be your guides. As concerned as we are about the multiplying risks in the world, we're equally excited by the better models for living we see emerging, ones we're helping to create with our direct participation.

It's time for action. To safeguard your future. To leave a better tomorrow to those you care about. To live more authentically and, most important, to find greater happiness.

It's time to *Prosper!*

In community, your authors:

CHAPTER 1

THE THREE ES

Before we get into the particulars of becoming more resilient, we'd like to share with you the data that explains why many people are increasingly motivated to action.

The short version is that virtually everything we take for granted is on an unsustainable trajectory. Our economic model demands perpetual growth – indefinitely. Exponentially increasing levels of debt, overuse of ecosystems, and ever-accelerating depletion of fossil fuels are just a few of the many examples of *practices that cannot continue forever.*

Stating the obvious: anything that can't go on forever, won't.

Now, before you quickly dismiss us as dyed-in-the-wool pessimists, allow us to step through the data that supports our views. Even if you're already well-versed in this material, you may find this re-grounding in the data as motivation to get busy on your path towards resilience.

Your authors are data driven people, and we track a lot of it very closely through the work at our website, PeakProsperity.com. What sets us apart from most commentators, analysts and observers is that we dig deep into what we call the **Three Es**—the Economy, Energy *and* the Environment - and connect them all into a single, simple, and coherent framework.

When new data emerges, we adjust our views accordingly. But with the facts available to us today, this is the story we have to tell.

ENERGY

It all begins with energy. You are so completely enveloped within the comforting embrace of surplus energy that it probably escapes your notice and proper appreciation. As water is to a fish, so energy is to you.

Take a moment and glance at the things around you. Walls and ceilings, lights, appliances, furniture and clothing. There are metals, plastics and fabrics galore all around you.

Think about where you drove yesterday. How far will you travel over the next month? Where are you headed later today?

Each and every one of the things you can see, touch or do in life got there or is made possible because of energy. Fossil fuel energy mainly—but even more specifically, because of **oil**. Ninety-five percent of everything that moves from point A to point B in our globalized, just-in-time economy does so because of liquid fuels derived from petroleum. This means that when you scanned your surroundings, virtually everything your eyes saw required oil to get there.

Widening beyond what you can see, at this very moment there are massive traffic jams on hundreds of highways in hundreds of cities across the globe. Twenty-four hours a day. Three hundred sixty-five days a year, during every hour of every day, there are millions of cars just sitting there, stuck in massive traffic jams.

The *price* of oil is sensitively dependent on whether we are consuming slightly more than we are producing (which causes the price to rise), or if we're consuming slightly less than we are producing (resulting in a price decline). But prices can distract you from the truth about oil, which is that we are constantly 24x7x365 burning it up in greater and greater amounts with every passing year.

Energy is also critically important because it's tightly linked to economic growth, which is revered and sought by every nation on the planet. Everybody wants *growth*, especially more economic growth, which means continuously having more things produced and sold this year than last.

But this slavish fixation on economic growth has led us to overlook the reality that, for every additional 1% increase in Gross Domestic Product (GDP), electricity usage increases by roughly 0.5% and oil use increases by roughly 0.25%. So, it's as simple as this: Growing an economy requires the consumption of energy to grow.

But this is clearly not a reasonable demand to make of a finite planet. While the demand for economic growth is *unlimited*, there's a limited amount oil in the ground. The same is true for other fossil fuels such as coal and natural gas.

Centering just on oil, because the world remains so tremendously dependent on it, there are only two things you need to know.

First, the easy stuff is all gone. If there were easy stuff left we would not be drilling in ultra-deep waters, fracking at enormous expense, and boiling tar residue off of Canadian sand. Getting oil out of the ground is undeniably and obviously getting harder and more expensive as time goes on.

Second, there are no viable replacements for cheap oil anywhere on the horizon, at least not at the scales required *. We have no plan B in place for how we are going to transition off of oil. *[*Note: the projected contributions from biofuels and electric vehicles are so tiny compared to oil's stronghold on the transportation sector that they can be all but ignored at the moment.]*

So as oil depletes, it becomes more expensive to extract every year, and we have no substitutes for it. Every year those two concepts become just a little bit more obvious.

The insidious part of this story is buried in the 'more expensive to extract' statement. Putting aside the additional money involved for a moment, what that really means is that we have to expend more energy to just get the same amount of energy out of the ground.

It takes energy to get energy, and we run both our economy and society on the *surplus energy* left over after all the energy used to find, extract, refine and distribute that energy has been subtracted.

Imagine for a moment that we were living in 1930 when those famous oil 'gushers' were being drilled. Back then we might have expended a single barrel of oil's worth of energy in order to get 100 barrels out of the ground. That surplus balance of 99 barrels of oil went to market, and the nation used it however it wished.

This oil could have been used frivolously, or to build up the nation's infrastructure. It could power the plowing of new farmland, or the import of feather boas from Brazil.

The point we're making here is this: our culture, our economy, our jobs —progress and society itself—all exist due to *surplus* energy. Whether the world can produce 100 million barrels of oil per day or just 50 million is far less relevant than how much *surplus* energy there is to support the rest of our complex economy and the way of life we consider to be normal.

Now suppose for a moment that you live 30 years in the future and all new oil discoveries return just 1.5 barrels of oil for every barrel expended to find, produce and deliver that oil to market. What kind of a world do you suppose that would be like? Instead of expending a barrel of oil and getting 99 barrels back like we did in 1930, we'd only get 0.5 barrels back.

What's the difference between 99 and 0.5? Night and day. Not everything that can be supported on 99 surplus barrels can be supported on a measly 0.5 barrels. In fact, we'd argue that practically everything we hold dear about our modern, comfortable lifestyles would vanish if we were suddenly forced to exist on a paltry 0.5 barrel surplus.

In rough terms, where the energy industry was once using 1% of our total annual energy and leaving 99% for society, it will someday be consuming 67%, leaving the rest of us to fight over the remaining 33%.

For those of us who have studied what life will look and feel like under these conditions, the answer is obvious. We will inherit a future defined by *less* of everything. The world will be a far less dynamic, less easy place to live with a much-simplified economy, reduced travel, and vastly fewer—or at least very *different*—opportunities compared to today. Unless you happen to work in the energy extraction business, in which case you may be very busy indeed trying to meet the demands of your increasingly-frustrated customers!

The sober truth is that we are well on that path of diminishing energy returns. The much-vaunted shale plays in the US you've seen touted in the media as the savior to the world's oil needs? Those deliver perhaps 8:1 to 5:1 net energy returns.

Put another way, in the past 85 years of oil production, we now find ourselves getting just *one-twentieth* the return as when we started. It's difficult to overstate the importance of this fact. It's an astonishing development touching on everything we hold dear and you should rightly be wondering why you are reading about it here and not on the front page of every major newspaper.

The trends clearly show that the diminishing energy returns of oil are a permanent feature. Plentiful, cheap oil was a once-in-a-species bonanza. We've been blowing through it as if it were a massive and self-replenishing party fund, and we've fashioned our entire way of life and all our plans for the future on the comforting but false belief that oil's age will never end.

The golden age of oil discoveries, you may be surprised to learn, peaked way back in the 1960's. In 2014, world discoveries of new oil reserves dropped to a 20-year low, marking the fourth consecutive year of discovery declines, and only replaced roughly one-sixth of what we burned during that same year.

At the time of this writing in spring of 2015, there are no serious efforts underway for a smooth transition to a new energy source after the oil is gone.

Should a credible transition plan ever be devised, it will ask much of society. Such an effort will require the sort of dedication brought to the moon project, multiplied by the constructive intensity that gave us the interstate highway system, multiplied by some large whole number like 10. Or maybe 100. The budget and manpower needed will be staggering. But as of now, those in the halls of power are not debating this. It's not even on their radar.

As for other forms of energy that might ride to the rescue, well, let's just say that the current levels of investment in alternative energy (solar, wind, hydro, etc) are not yet equal to the task. Although energy production from alternative sources has been advancing nicely, it's swamped each year by the gross increase in additional fossil fuel use. It's an unfair race where fossil fuels have a gigantic head start.

More importantly, wind and solar are not replacements for oil. Oil gives us transportation fuels and chemical feed stocks while wind and solar give us electrons. They are not interchangeable inputs given the transportation industrial infrastructure we currently have.

As the surplus energy we receive from oil and other fossil fuels dwindles (the same dynamic is happening in coal and natural gas, too, albeit on a different timeline), we're going to have to get used to getting by with less, because we will be able to do less. This will impact our lifestyles over the next several decades, affecting some harder and more quickly than others. (As we often say: your local mileage will vary).

But one thing we all care about is extremely vulnerable to a decline in surplus energy: the economy. Remember when we talked earlier about all that economic growth our corporate and political leaders are so fixated on? Perhaps it's time to be asking what will happen to it when there's not enough surplus energy left over to dedicate to growth.

This completes a (very) brief tour of energy, which will allow us to better appreciate the economy, the next "E" in our story. Trust us, this is important information that is leading somewhere.

ECONOMY

The economy is an easy thing to explain. While some describe it as the complicated sum of all the products and services a region produces, that's a definition of what it *is*. In terms of what it *does*, the best explanation is that *it grows*.

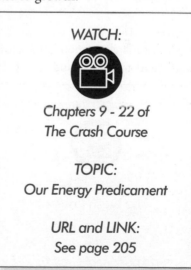

WATCH:

Chapters 9 - 22 of
The Crash Course

TOPIC:
Our Energy Predicament

URL and LINK:
See page 205

We like our economy to grow by some percentage over time (be that a quarter, a year or a decade), which means that it is growing *exponentially*. This is a hugely important idea so let's spend a bit of time developing the concept.

Anything that is growing by some percentage over some unit of time is growing exponentially. It could be a single percent (1%) each year or it could be 5% per month. It doesn't matter by how much or for how long, all that matters is that this thing we're measuring is growing by some percentage over time.

You've heard about this phenomenon endlessly, perhaps without realizing it. The newspapers and televisions constantly repeat the data points: Car sales are up 12% this month. House sales are up 5% year over year. The economy has grown by 3.2% this quarter.

If you look carefully, you'll see that each of these is actually referring to *a percentage increase over a unit of time* – which means that the things we most carefully measure, track and report to ourselves are all growing *exponentially*.

So why is it so important to understand the concept of exponential growth? Because it is literally going to kill us if we don't. We need to understand exponential growth because we are completely surrounded by it, and appreciating that will help us to both understand what's happening today as well as predict what's coming tomorrow.

"The greatest shortcoming of the human race is our inability to understand the exponential function"

—Albert Bartlett

Unfortunately, exponential growth is not an intuitive concept. We're hard-wired to understand direct, linear relationships. We can hit a fastball, but slipping on ice surprises us. No matter how fast the ball is thrown it's moving at a constant speed, while gravity accelerates exponentially. Exponential rates of change confuse most of us except for a very few well-trained mathematicians; so please don't be put off by any doubts you may have about fully grasping this concept.

Fortunately, there are some relatable ways to understand how critical exponential growth is to our economy—one very good one is presented in the chapter on

WATCH:

Chapter 3 of
The Crash Course

TOPIC:
Exponential Growth

URL and LINK:
See page 205

Exponential Growth within our online video series, *The Crash Course*. If you haven't yet seen it, it's worth taking a few minutes to watch it now, if you're able to (it's only six minutes in length). It really makes the concept easy to grasp.

Another good one is the Rule of 72, which works like this:

Suppose we said that we wanted our economy to grow by 5% per year. The Rule of 72 allows us to quickly answer the question: *How long will it be before our economy has fully doubled in size?*

To answer that question all we have to do is divide the rate of growth into 72. While 5% doesn't sound like very much growth, the Rule of 72 tells us that in just 14.4 years (= 72/5) an economy growing at 5% per year will be twice as large.

As in "fully doubled" in just 14.4 years!

Everything will be twice as big: twice as much economic activity, twice as many cars sold, twice as much food grown and eaten, twice as many airline miles travelled and trips taken—everything will be two times bigger.

Imagine you live in a small city that is growing by this modest 5% per year and you have a child. Before that child's 15th birthday, your small city now has twice as much of everything. By the time that child has almost reached her 29th birthday, the city in which she was born will now be 4 times as large because it has gone through two doublings. If the growth persists, by the time your child is 58 years old, her small city will be 16 times as large as when she was born. More frighteningly, just 14.4 years after that, at the ripe old age of 72, the city will now be 32 times as large. 32 *times!*

If that same economy were to grow at 7.2%, the current reported rate of China's GDP growth, then that economy would double every 10 years.

Do you see the predicament here yet? If every economy in the world is growing exponentially, and they are all doubling away every decade or two, eventually they'll run out of resources and room. That's just common sense, right?

The world is already mired in low growth and saddled with some $200 trillion of debt, up a whopping $57 trillion just since 2007. Sadly, the world didn't take on all that new debt because of clear-eyed confidence in the future, but because worried politicians borrowed it from scared central bankers, both of whom merely wanted to the keep the whole system from imploding.

The core of the problem, never publicly recognized by either the politicians or central planners, is that our system of money and our banking and financial systems are all hopelessly addicted to exponentially growing piles of debt and money. As long as they are growing exponentially, everything is stable, but the minute they stagnate or shrink(!), as happened in 2009 after the real estate bust, the financial and banking systems threaten to collapse.

Does having monetary and financial systems whose very stability are built around the idea of perpetual exponential expansion sound particularly robust or intelligent? If it doesn't, then you are on the same wavelength as your authors.

Okay, we've got just one more topic to cover before we can assemble this all into a coherent call to action.

ENVIRONMENT

Even at today's level of world economic output, there are already hundreds of flashing warning signs saying that we're taking too much *from* the natural world and putting too much waste *back in* to it.

The "plan" of every single one of the world's leaders is to double the rate of economic output of their country, and then double it again. Forever. But as we can all deduce, it's not possible to endlessly double the size of something contained within a fixed space.

> WATCH:
>
>
>
> Chapters 6 - 18 of
> The Crash Course
>
> TOPIC:
> The Risks to our Economy
>
> URL and LINK:
> See page 205

The world is very big, but it is not infinite. This is the reality that the generations alive today have to confront. However difficult it proves, either practically or emotionally, we are the first ones in history who are going to slam into the Earth's limits to growth.

It's not going to be possible to double the rate at which oil currently comes out of the ground. And even if it were, climate scientists tell us that would be a terrible idea. Certainly ocean fish stocks are not going to double anytime soon; they're in full-blown collapse as it is. Nor are we going to double the water taken from depleted aquifers, or the food from rapidly-depleting soils. We may be able to eek out a little bit more from these stressed systems for a few more years but that bought time will come with a terrible cost.

Wedged between an energy system that cannot possibly expand forever, and an economic model that demands endless expansion, we have clear, ominous, troubling evidence—mountains of it!—that humans are impacting the natural world in destructive ways that will result in disruptive changes and ecosystem collapse.

Biological diversity is the very foundation of the natural world. In times past a human could live an entire life lasting 80 years and, on average, experience one species extinction during their lifetime. Now we are losing, on average, several species *per day* by some estimates (or several hundred per day, by others).

More than half of the world's major aquifers are now in a state of dangerous depletion, and the millions to billions of people who depend upon them have no alternative supplies to draw upon.

Fertile soils are being degraded and eroded such that we can calculate when they will be entirely gone. Under current farming practices we may have as few as 60 to 100 harvests left. No soil means no food means no humans.

The oceans are acidifying at the fastest pace in 300 million years. We know that the largest mass extinction in Earth's history, the Permian extinction, the one that erased more than 90% of all life forms in the oceans and on land, happened because the oceans acidified too much and too fast.

Climate change is now a matter of scientific record. The only questions left are how extreme it will be and how much damage we will experience. The glaciers in Antarctica are calving off at an accelerating pace, and their hundreds of gigatons of inertia will carry them into the sea, raising ocean levels, no matter what we do.

In response to these existential threats, most of the responsible nations are doing little more than making soothing noises publicly, while continuing with 'business as usual' in the background. Talk is cheap, but real solutions will be among the most expensive and radical tasks ever undertaken in human history. Our entire food and energy production systems will have to be re-engineered. Our species will have to convert from being wanton consumers of natural resources to responsible *stewards* of them. Where and how we live, how we transport ourselves, how we transact, and how we interact with nature—all will have to change dramatically.

The big question is: *Will those changes be on our terms, or other terms?* With each passing year that the human race ignores or delays action, the answer being 'other terms' continue to increase.

Okay, thank you for sticking with us this far. Take a deep breath and let out whatever tension you are carrying. Here's where it all comes together.

THE THREE Es

Now you know why we believe that all three Es must be viewed at once. They're so interconnected we can't simply address one without impacting the others. So to the extent that central bankers are busy pulling monetary levers while ignoring the trends in the environment and energy sectors is the extent to which they are making grave errors.

Add up all the Three Es and you see we have:

1. an economy that must expand, connected to
2. an energy system that cannot expand, all wrapped up in
3. an environment that is both being depleted of resources and saturated with pollutants.

The inescapable conclusion to all this? Things are going to change. Big time.

At Peak Prosperity, we remind ourselves with the punchline: *The next 20 years are going to be completely unlike the past 20 years.* Never before has humanity had to deal with such a massive set of intertwined predicaments (problems have solutions; predicaments only have outcomes that need to be prepared for). We simply don't have any relevant history to inform our decision-making here.

This means we can't count on the cavalry to ride to our rescue and make these issues disappear. That's just not going to happen given the number and scope of the challenges we face. Instead we, as individuals, are each going to need to prepare for a very different and quite possibly turbulent future.

Our old habits and assumptions will conspire to steer us wrong in most cases. But by focusing on developing *resilience*, we can dramatically increase our chances of mastering whatever rules the coming future will require us to live by.

In short, it's time to get ready. That's where the rest of this book comes in.

CHAPTER 2

RESILIENCE: WHAT IS IT, EXACTLY?

The main theme of this book is that *resilience* is the key to prosperity. We like this word because it covers a lot of territory, but it can mean a lot of different things to different people depending on their age, location, wealth, or health. So it's worth taking a moment to define what we mean by 'resilience' in order to make sure we share a common understanding.

The Oxford dictionary definition offers a good place to start:

---

re·sil·ience
noun

1. the ability of a substance or object to spring back into shape; elasticity.

2. the capacity to recover quickly from difficulties; toughness.

We all know people who are able to bounce back quickly from illness and others who aren't. This is an example of resilience in health. But resilience also applies to nearly every aspect of our lives: to an investment portfolio, a home, a garden, a career, or a personal relationship.

Each of these things is said to be more resilient if it is able to weather stormy times (literally or figuratively) well.

To the textbook definition we can also add the concept of *redundancy*. Nature teaches us that resilience means having multiple ways of meeting any particular need.

Laying several eggs in a nest instead of just one is an example of resilience through redundancy. So is the demonstrated ability of Central Park squirrels to eat anything from acorns to cheese popcorn to hot dogs as compared to the giant panda which can only eat one food type, bamboo. Squirrels breed rapidly, pandas rarely. You might have noticed, there are a lot more squirrels than pandas in the world.

Similarly, wetlands can absorb a lot more water than a concrete ditch because wetlands have untold crevices and layers of spongy material. They act as a natural backup water storage system for storing the rains when they come.

Extending nature's cue to our home, we note that having several methods and systems involved in heating and cooling your house makes you more resilient because you're able to switch across energy fuel types if one becomes scarce or expensive. As an example, you could heat with gas, wood, and passive solar design, and cool with A/C and better window shades. Even better, reduce your need for heating and cooling by investing in thicker insulation throughout your home. With a hybrid system like this, you'll spend less over the long haul and be able to more easily meet your family's needs compared to someone who hasn't made these investments.

So to the dictionary definition of resilience, we add:

3. Having multiple, redundant means of meeting one's needs; having buffers and stored resources; and the ability to switch easily between different potential solutions.

This means that resilience cuts against our current so-called 'modern' or 'superior' way of life because so much of the developed world lifestyle revolves around micro-specialization, lean inventories, and just-in-time fulfillment. While dazzlingly cost efficient when everything goes as planned, these approaches are vulnerable to unexpected disruptions. Did you know that most cities only have between three and five days worth of food on hand in their grocery stores? If for any reason the constant stream of trucks resupplying those stores should halt, as happened to coastal New Jersey when Hurricane Sandy hit in 2012, then shortages, hunger, and social unrest can quickly follow.

Take a moment to ask yourself what items in your life you're counting on being there in the future, especially in times of need. What would happen to you if they weren't? How resilient *are* you?

THE 8 PRINCIPAL FORMS OF RESILIENCE

If your answer is *Not as resilient as I'd like to be*, don't worry. Nearly everyone else on the planet is in the same boat. What matters more, what's truly going to decide your fate, are the steps you take from here on out.

Which is why we've created this book. It provides tangible, practical guidance on exactly how to build greater resilience into your life.

But first, you need a more detailed, concrete understanding of the principal component parts of resilience.

We're going to use a framework inspired by the work of AppleSeed Permaculture's Ethan Roland and Gregory Landua (http://www.regenterprise.com), as well as the work of coaching pioneer Thomas Leonard, which we've modified to fit the purposes of this book. The framework is based on the observation that, for humans, resilience is attained through the build up of resources and capabilities—referred to in aggregate as capital – across 8 discrete categories of life. This capital has real value, and the capital in one category can usually be exchanged for capital in another. We'll explain this idea further in a moment, just note for now that it's an important feature.

Thinking of these components as capital to be earned, exchanged and invested is a very helpful—and ultimately very accurate—way to mentally understand the larger concept of resilience.

8 FORMS OF CAPITAL

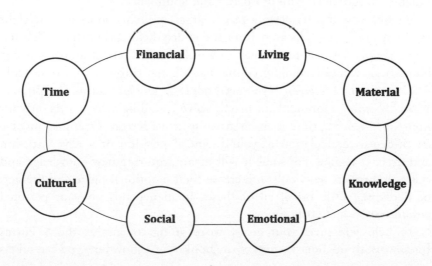

Financial capital is the one with which most people are most intuitively familiar. It's our money, our stock and bond portfolios, the income we receive from our jobs, and our expenses and debts.

Social capital involves our private and public relationships. These are the relationships that nourish and guide us, the less intimate relationships we have with people with whom we exchange favors, and the connections that we can draw upon to meet our needs and offer our goods and services.

Living capital is the land, the trees, the water, the soil, and the animals around us. It's our bodies as well – our health, fitness level, and physical abilities.

Material capital refers to tangible possessions such as homes, bridges, building materials, tools, stored food, computers, solar arrays, and cars.

Knowledge capital includes the things that we know and our expertise in applying that knowledge.

Emotional and spiritual capital is measured by our personal capacity to roll with the punches, to weather inner storms and outer dramas while remaining calm and centered.

Cultural capital is defined by the stories, songs, and habits of the local population we live among. Some communities react well to adversity and some do not. The difference is a measure of the cultural capital of each.

And finally we have **time** as a form of capital, which refers to the precious, ever-depleting commodity that we need to allocate wisely if we wish to inhabit a future filled with prosperity and abundance.

We like how this framework places equal emphasis on each of its eight components. It steers us away from the widely held and untrue belief that if you simply have a lot of money, or a well-stocked retreat property in the boondocks, you can handle anything that life may throw at you. To be truly resilient—to be *prosperous*—you need depth in all eight forms of capital.

So becoming more resilient may involve installing solar panels on your house, or spending time at an intensive spiritual retreat. Or it may involve an in-depth recalculation of your financial position or a new nutrition and exercise regime. For some it will mean acquiring new knowledge and skills, and others new tools to increase their emotional range and literacy, or perhaps a little bit of all of these. It all depends on your personal circumstances and goals

To help you meet your goals, we're going to employ the 8 Forms framework throughout the rest of the book. We'll show how you can take a form of capital that you happen to have in relative abundance and exchange it for a form of capital that you lack. What might this look like? Perhaps using your professional expertise to create a second income stream, or trading money for compost. Again, your personal situation will define the specifics of the course you take.

To help you chart that course, we have dedicated a full chapter to each of the eight forms, filled with insights and best practices we've collected on how to build capital in each. All you need to do is follow the steps.

INSUFFICIENT BUT NECESSARY

When it comes to these steps, many of the individual ones you take will likely feel insufficient in and of themselves, yet it's important to understand that they are *necessary* in aggregate.

For instance, swapping out the incandescent bulbs in your house for LED lights is completely insufficient to shift the larger trend of global warming. But, if all households do this, across many nations, a material impact will be made and therefore it's necessary.

Likewise, storing extra food may be totally insufficient to feed your family for more than a few days or weeks. But it's necessary that you do it anyways, because it might make all the difference in the wake of a natural disaster.

We're going to recommend dozens of things, each of which may strike you as insufficient by themselves. Together, however, they're completely necessary for prosperity, peace of mind, aligning your thoughts and actions effectively, and providing motivation to those who may look to you for guidance and leadership.

A JOURNEY, NOT A DESTINATION

We heartily recommend that you begin preparing as early as possible. The crises headed our way will be with us for a very long time, which means that becoming resilient is not a "one and done" objective.

The need to remain resilient will likely increase as the Three E trends arrive in force over next few decades, and the type of resilience required of us will likely shift as developments unfold.

In short: think of developing resilience as a journey rather than a destination.

In whichever areas of your life you choose to focus your efforts, ask yourself three basic questions:

1. **What should I keep doing?** Most of the things you already have in your life you are going to keep. Most of the things you already do, you are going to keep doing. Eating well, getting plenty of sleep, laughing and loving your family are all examples of things you are going to keep doing. It's important to emphasize this because some people look at the changes coming and think we're talking about having to drop everything and start a brand new, and less enjoyable life. In truth, 80% to 90% of the things that are already in your life will remain there.

2. **What should I stop doing?** Some things no longer make sense given the macro trends in play, and you should stop doing them right away because they no longer serve you or are increasing your expenditures and risks. Unearth the things you're doing that you should stop. Stop eating foods that don't nourish you. Stop wasting money, energy and other resources – especially time.

3. **What new things should I start doing?** Here's where the magic begins. What are all the *new* things you need to do to align your actions with the new reality of the world around you? Depending on your circumstances and aspirations, you may start exercising more, or begin new practices of daily awareness and connection. Perhaps it's time to get to know your neighbors better, or learn how to garden. We'll help you figure out which ones to focus on first.

But keep in mind that your pursuit of all of these will be fluid. Some you'll handle quickly; others may take years to get right. Just remember it's a journey, and enjoy the progress you make while on it.

MIND THE GAP!

Taking these steps is also very important for emotional reasons.

If you ride the British tube, or subway, you'll have heard the pleasant recording of a woman's voice and/or noticed the signs telling you to 'mind the gap.' In this case the gap being referred to is a dangerous empty spot between the train and the platform.

Another anxiety-producing gap exists between what people *value* and what they *do*. The two are often not always aligned in our modern culture. In that gap between one's thoughts and one's actions is where anxiety and fear live and breed. Sometimes in debilitating, paralyzing amounts.

If you *know* that an earthquake is a distinct possibility where you live, and yet have *done nothing* to prepare, then you have a gap. Even if you don't spend much time consciously dwelling on it, an uneasy situation has merely been suppressed and sits there, quietly gnawing at the edges of your consciousness, corroding your overall sense of well-being.

Add up enough of these gaps and you'll end up more anxious and unsettled than you need to be. In our work, we often encounter people who are anxious or depressed without understanding why. Fortunately, in most cases the anxiety and stress can be relieved by simply closing the gap with a few simple actions—in our previous example, it might be as simple as putting together an earthquake response kit. Unfortunately, a lot of people won't undertake even the simplest of steps.

Another example is that our just-in-time food delivery system could suffer a breakdown for any one of a dozen legitimate reasons. As mentioned, most cities and communities have only 3-4 days of food in the stores. A lot of people comfort themselves with the knowledge that the stores have never run dry before. Therefore a prolonged period without access to groceries seems far too remote a possibility to concern themselves with.

However we know that the fear of shortage lurks because every time there's an approaching hurricane or big snow storm, people flock to the stores and load up "just in case." Well, just in case of what? The answer is, on some level, everybody knows that losing access to food during a disaster is a possibility that can't be entirely dismissed.

There that knowledge sits, just out of sight, like an unwanted guest until an approaching storm wakes it up and brings it to the surface. So what can we do about it? That's easy; buy some extra long-term storage food that will last for 30 years without needing any additional attention and kick that worry right out of your brain. Your authors did exactly that a number of years ago, and the sense of peace it bought has paid itself back many times over compared to the relatively minor expense of the actual food.

Even better, there's no way to lose. If we've concerned ourselves over a risk that never materializes (hopefully!) and we never have to actually use that stored food, then we'll donate it to a food bank or other worthy outlet in three decades. We get to feel good about the donation and maybe even take a tax deduction in the process. No matter how you slice it, in terms of reduced anxiety, effort or money, it wasn't wasted effort.

So our advice here is simple: if you want to reduce your fears, anxiety or concern about the future, don't just sit there, do something!

SELFLESS NOT SELFISH

Another objection we hear to the prospect of preparing and becoming more resilient is that those actions could be seen as being selfish. Instead we see them as being self*less*. Those who are not prepared when an emergency strikes are a drain on critical resources, while those who are prepared can be of assistance.

To be among those who can be in a position to render assistance, or at least need none of their own, means that your prior acts of preparation have selflessly removed you from the minus column and placed you on the plus side.

The first steps towards preparedness usually involve addressing your own needs or those of your loved ones, but many people then go beyond that and prepare for others who may not be able to do so, or have not done so, or maybe even will *not* do so.

But let us put an important qualifier on that; preparing *before* a crisis hits is responsible and selfless, but trying to accumulate necessary items *during* a crisis is an act of hoarding. **We do not and never will advocate hoarding.** Responsible preparations begin long before any trouble appears. Anything else stands a good chance of making things worse, not better.

The news has been full of stories of how people behave when scarcity strikes and they are generally not pretty. People in Boston fought over bottled water just hours after a water main broke in 2010. Nasty fights, too.

In Venezuela, as of the writing of this book, desperate people are attempting to buy anything and everything that might remain in the stores as their national currency devalues by the day. This is bringing forth all sorts of government-mandated counter measures that make it impossible for many families to buy essential items.

We mentioned earlier that time may well be your most valuable asset in becoming resilient. Be aware that many things that are easily available now may be difficult to obtain later. Now, before any big crises have hit, it's very easy to pick up the phone, or click a mouse button, and have the big brown truck of happiness roll up to your doorstep a few days later. Everything you could ever want to buy is currently available and stores are abundantly stocked in most countries. However, we can imagine a large number of possible futures where such easy access to consumer goods and desired items is either much more difficult or impossible.

WHAT RESILIENCE IS **NOT**

In closing, it's worth clarifying a few things that resilience is *not*.

Sometimes people think that our encouragement of becoming resilient is the same thing as being a "prepper" or survivalist. While we might recommend a few of the same items that you'd find in a prepper's house, that's where the similarity ends.

Our version of resilience and preparedness has nothing to do with living in fear, merely hoping to survive. It's about thriving today—and tomorrow—*whatever* the future brings.

Being prepared, or resilient, is something that any prudent adult can and should aspire to. Like a boat captain who assures that his ship is properly equipped with a working radio, life vests, and life rafts, each of us can and should do the same for our own households.

And just as we'd never accuse a captain with proper safety equipment of being a pessimist or a crackpot hoping his boat will someday sink, it's equally inappropriate to cast efforts towards resilience as somehow being unbalanced. To us, the exact opposite is true. Those who refuse to take even minimal efforts towards securing their own futures are exposing themselves and those around them to unnecessary risks.

Think of it like carrying fire insurance on a home. That's socially acceptable, is considered prudent, and nobody ever implies that the owner of home who carries fire insurance is secretly hoping that their home burns down.

Now that we know what resilience is, and what it is not, let's move deeper.

CHAPTER 3

RESILIENCE —
WHY DOES IT MATTER?

As we look at the global predicaments laid out in Chapter 2—The Three Es—it's natural to wonder: *How did we get here?*

The reasons are numerous—resource exploitation, population expansion, a profound societal disconnection from nature, short-term thinking, to name just a few—but the underlying cause is the same: our never-ending pursuit of *growth*.

A FAILED NARRATIVE

Research shows that it's the stories we tell ourselves that guide and determine our destiny. And we, as a global society, have near-universally embraced a narrative that says "*More is Better!*" about practically every aspect of life.

Financially, we're told that having more money is better than having less. At the national level, we've constructed an economy that *must* grow in order to function well—and so our politicians and captains of industry constantly agitate for *more* GDP and *more* job growth. To feed this growth, more and more debt is created each year. Energetically, this drives countries around the world in a race to extract more barrels of oil and other fossil fuels out of the ground. It's the same with mineral ores, with bushels of food harvested, with fishery hauls, with new houses built, new cars manufactured, new smart phones sold, and on and on…

This narrative of "ever more" is coded deep within our ancestry. It served our hunter-gatherer ancestors well, as they lived under conditions of much greater resource scarcity than most humans today. Securing more calories, or more sexual mates, often determined the survival of both the person and their progeny. It continued to serve the human race well as we developed agriculture and began to industrialize. At least, for as long as civilizations had access to untapped resources.

But in today's world where there are no more undiscovered continents and the concentration of remaining resources is becoming increasingly dilute, we are the first living generation to encounter limits to growth on a planetary scale. We no longer live in a world where our narrative of endless growth is possible, let alone desirable.

And as the global resources pie no longer expands as it once did, competition for the slices that remain intensifies—especially with overall world population still growing. If history is any guide (and we think it is), increased competition for resources will lead to friction between nations, social classes, and demographic groups alike—discord that is becoming ever more apparent, as those adhering to the old narrative find themselves increasingly unfulfilled and frustrated.

A good example of this is the wide-scale rejection of cultural norms the millennial generation is demonstrating (those born between the early 1980s and early 2000s). Facing a tough job market (the unemployment rate of millennials in the United States is double that of the overall population) that offers low wages and little employer loyalty, sky-high education costs resulting in record student debt balances, and over-inflated housing prices making first-time home buying unaffordable, many are simply "opting out." They are—consciously or unconsciously— under-enthused to blindly follow the American Dream recipe of: go to school, get a job, get married, buy a house, and consume, consume, consume! Many rightly see this instead as a recipe for lifelong debt serfdom, especially when they're also being asked to pay for the excessive debts and unfunded entitlements racked up by the generations that preceded them. Oh yes, and all while inheriting a national infrastructure that is quite literally falling apart.

Is it any mystery then why millennials are much less able, let alone interested and willing, to make major purchases (car, home, etc), get married, have children, or work a standard 9-to-5 corporate job as previous cohorts their same age?

We see similar pressure brewing between the haves and the have-nots. Across the world, the wealth gap between the rich and poor has rarely been as extreme as it is now. Remember that competition for pie slices? Well, as the pie itself stops getting bigger, those in power use their authority and influence to keep their share of the pie growing for as long as possible afterwards. This results in less and less for everyone else.

We can see direct evidence of this reality in the dramatic jump in wealth disparity that has happened since the 2008 financial crisis. For a few years, the credit pie stopped growing—and what happened? The response engineered by our governments directed trillions of new dollars into the asset classes owned by the already-rich, resulting in a robust boost to their portfolio values while the rest of the 99% has been left to simply watch and struggle onwards.

The outbreak of protest the world saw during the Occupy Wall Street movement of 2009-2011 was an immediate reaction to the unfairness of this class dichotomy. We are likely to see this pattern again, this time with more vitriol and violence, as the wealth gap grows further.

There's a similar dynamic at the geopolitical level. A general East vs. West tension is brewing as developing nations increasingly look to wrest resources from the clutches of the OECD members, whom they understandably argue have consumed more than their fair share over the past several centuries.

The key conclusion to draw here is that, as the Club of Rome predicted in the 1970s, modern civilization is finally encountering the limits of a finite planet. If that's indeed the case—which we hope *The Crash Course* and our related works empirically show it is—then our societal "growth = goodness" narrative is no longer enabling for us. In fact, it is now dangerous and destructive to our well-being, as its continued pursuit will only accelerate the drawdown of remaining resources and exacerbate the resulting conflicts.

Our warning is this: if we do not adopt a new narrative, the destructive status quo will continue…until the point it simply can't. When that moment abruptly arrives, our entire system of living will break. At that point, we'll be forced to make do with *less*—whether we like it or not—and our options for moving forward will be much more limited than they are now.

The first step towards achieving long-term sustainable prosperity is, of course, to *adopt a better narrative*. A narrative of living within our means, of resource stewardship, and of finding happiness in a life of purpose, not of possessions.

We don't think it's realistic to expect our leaders and social institutions to make this mindset shift on their own before calamity arrives. There are just too many people who are invested (emotionally, financially and otherwise) in continuing the status quo for as long as possible. As Upton Sinclair wrote "*It is difficult to get a man to understand something, when his salary depends upon his not understanding it,*" and all evidence since the last financial crisis shows that if the establishment can deny, ignore or delay dealing with problems, it will.

This is why we urge individuals like you to develop a mindset of resilience. You can make changes to your lifestyle now, before the next crisis, that will greatly reduce your vulnerability—while quite likely, boosting your quality of life at the same time. And when the whole house of cards comes tumbling down at some future point, you'll be fine, as you've already acclimated to and learned to enjoy a low-input lifestyle. As our friend the archdruid John Michael Greer cheekily puts it: *Collapse now and avoid the rush.*

The rest of this book, and the workbook that accompanies it, will walk you through the details on how to prepare for tomorrow's "de-growth" today.

WHEN? WHEN? DEAR GOD, WHEN???

When is this collapse going to happen? is a question we get asked all the time. If we only knew with certainty, we could make a mint. Sigh…

We don't know. And neither does anyone else, by the way, which is why we deal in probabilities, not absolute forecasts.

The reality is that the collapse is happening right now, all around us. It is just happening at such a slow rate that people not consciously paying attention tend to miss it. You can see it in rising grocery prices, increasing political rhetoric between major powers, ice shelves calving at unprecedented rates, acidifying oceans, and depleting oil reserves.

As a scientist, Chris learned through years of study and observation that complex systems under stress tend to resist change until they reach a breaking point, and then they alter their state very quickly. The actual moment this trigger occurs is nearly impossible to predict, as physicist Per Bak demonstrated in the mid-1980s through his work involving the power-laws of self-organizing systems—most memorably by drizzling grains of sand onto a sand-pile. At some point, adding too much sand causes an avalanche that reverts the pile back to a lower-energy state. But as each individual grain is dropped onto the pile, current science has no way to predict its impact with mathematical certainty. Will it be the grain that triggers the avalanche? There's just no way of knowing.

But, Bak's work *did* prove that the odds of a major avalanche occurring increase with the number of grains added to the pile. More pointedly, as each sand grain was added, the pile would begin to accumulate larger areas of steepness, which he termed "fingers of instability." The more of these fingers of instability, the greater the chance that the next grain would trigger a collapse, and the greater the chance the collapse would be a large one.

The complex economic and resource-based systems we rely on operate similarly. They will resist change until a final stress, a final grain of sand falls, and then they rather suddenly and dramatically will shift to a brand new state. The relationship Bak observed has been found to exist throughout nature: in the sun's activity, in the movement of current through a resistor, and in the flow of rivers, to name just a few.

Take our financial markets as another example. If stock prices have been growing much faster than earnings and the underlying economy (which has been the case since 2009), and if the market has not experienced a correction of 10% or more for an extended period of time (as of this writing, the U.S. stock market has not dropped more than 10% for nearly 1,000 consecutive trading days—the 3rd longest such stretch in its history), then we can express confidence that the next correction will arrive sooner, and be greater, than historically average.

And when you add in all of the other potential risk factors we look at (exponential resource depletion, exponential credit growth, exponential population growth, etc.), we are able to draw similar conclusions that large systemic shocks are highly likely to materialize within the next few decades. Quite possibly sooner.

Not that we predict that one night we'll go to bed and wake up living in a *Hunger Games*-style dystopia. Rather, as is common with natural systems, we expect to see a series of smaller shocks and failures manifesting over time. In totality, the sum impact of these will be enormous. But the individual insults themselves likely won't feel transformative as they occur, though we're careful to add that local mileage may vary (meaning: different localities and populations will feel each impact with different intensities). We visualize this progression as akin to a bowling ball falling down a staircase. Each sudden jolt is then followed by a period of stability, albeit at a lower state. Things normalize, and then—*Thunk!*—the ball drops again.

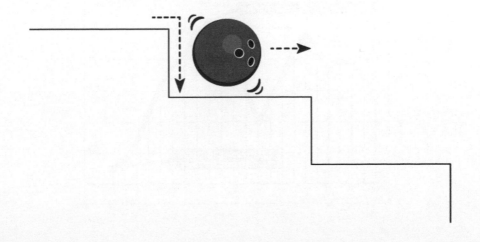

James Howard Kunstler aptly named this drawn-out collapse as *The Long Emergency*. John Michael Greer refers to it as *The Long Descent*. Either moniker works for us; the point is that we should prepare for a series of variable changes, not just a single seismic one.

And after each change, we'll have lost a little of what was possible before. Things will normalize around a new, simpler, baseline. We already have a number of examples of this. Take the nation of Greece, for instance. Before 2010, the people of Greece were able to do an awful lot more than they can do now. They built new infrastructure (construction for the 2004 Athens Olympics alone topped 8.5 billion Euros), had one of the most generous national pension programs, and had an unemployment rate in the single digits. Today in 2015, now that creditors have become fed-up with the staggering debt the country has amassed, the Greeks live under a fiscal austerity regime on par with the U.S. Great Depression of the 1930s.

The number of those living in poverty and homelessness has spiked, the unemployment rate has tripled to 25% (over 50% for workers under 25 years of age!), and business are shuttering at the rate of roughly 60 per day. To underscore our point: all this didn't happen overnight, instead it steadily worsened over several years. But the end result is crystal clear: much of what was possible in Greece just a half-decade ago is but a distant memory today.

We see the same dynamic playing out in our oceans, with collapsing fishery stocks and the rise of acidification levels. Here's a chart of the collapse of the Pacific sardine population, one of the base pillars of the food chain for the world's largest ocean:

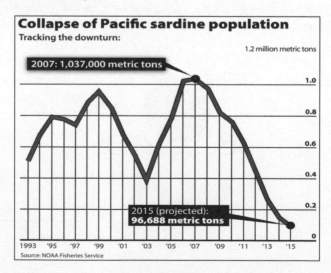

Collapse of Pacific sardine population
Tracking the downturn:

2007: 1,037,000 metric tons

1.2 million metric tons

2015 (projected): 96,688 metric tons

Source: NOAA Fisheries Service

Just eight years ago, the sardine population was measured at a multi-decade high. But each subsequent year since, more fish were harvested than were replenished. Each individual year didn't in itself look like a collapse; but now that we can view the past decade in its totality, the severity of the situation becomes immediately visible.

In this way, and in a multiplying number of others, we and our planet are experiencing a "death by a thousand cuts" as key supports for the economic, energy and environmental systems upon which we depend fail on our watch.

REALIZING IT'S ALL ABOUT POSITIVITY, NOT FEAR

Understandably, it's hard for most people not to react to this information without anxiety.

After all, in many ways it's a story of loss, which means it's about being unable to continue practices we've been accustomed to for our entire lives. So, emotions of fear, worry and grieving are in many ways to be expected by those new to this material.

We too experienced these feelings, along with healthy doses of anger and depression, in our early days of coming to terms with the data. With the experience of our own journeys of processing through this material, as well as helping thousands of others (millions, if we include our website) with the same, we've come to realize that this emotional path follows a similar progression as Elizabeth Kübler-Ross' Five Stages of Grief model. This makes perfect sense, as folks are essentially wrestling with the death of a dream, of a dearly-held belief of what the future was *supposed* to be.

But at the beginning, before they've successfully gone through these five stages, most folks find themselves living with a sense of existential dread. They describe themselves as feeling unfulfilled, unhappy, and powerless. This often creates a paralysis of despair which breeds inaction because, *Hey, why bother? We're all doomed anyways.*

If this sounds in any way like you, take heart. There is a good reason you're feeling this way (and, no, it's not because things are hopeless). What you're reacting to, possibly on an unconscious level, is the realization that the system itself is unsustainable and, as such, is destroying itself—for all of the reasons itemized in Chapter 2 and in *The Crash Course*, or perhaps additional ones you've observed in your own surroundings. Simply put: it doesn't feel good to participate in such a system.

Our observation of thousands of people like you have convinced us that when your actions are out of alignment with what you know to be true, we can predict two things.

The first is that fear takes residence in that gap between the actions you're taking and the actions you know you *should* be taking. Deep down, you know that denying reality only delays its arrival and magnifies its impact. That gnawing in your gut when you're charging more expenses to a credit card you know you should be paying off instead? That's the kind of angst we're talking about. But worse. For many, putting on a suit each day, fighting traffic on the commute to and from work, and living a frenetic consume-and-spend lifestyle feels increasingly like a sacrilege they'll be punished for as the post-peak-resources era arrives in force.

The other important development is that your integrity becomes compromised, and that feels awful. The simple morality all children are born with rebels within us when we engage in behavior we know to be wrong, triggering self-rebuking feelings of guilt, cognitive dissonance, and regret. If you truly believe that the system in which you live is destructive to both yourself and everybody else, then continuing to live and operate within the rules of that same system is self-harming. The mind rebels, and often forces itself to dissociate from this contradiction. As a result, since your consciousness is ignoring the issue, it manifests elsewhere as stress, depression, health issues, etc.

This duality of fear and compromised integrity is toxic to our health and happiness. Yet we see it all around us. In the 80% of Californians living in homes not inspected or retrofitted for earthquake resistance. In the millions of Texans and Pennsylvanians permitting natural gas fracking in their counties, despite the resulting contamination of their groundwater. In the millions of American workers annually at risk of losing their jobs due to automation and off-shoring, who are not taking steps now to re-train for a more secure role. Clearly, there's a widely shared human trait of ignoring an existential risk above a certain magnitude. Yet the long-term cost of such behavior may prove to be as high as the feared injury.

But it doesn't have to be this way! And here is where we get to the heart of this chapter: *Why resilience is so important.* In the natural world, it is the resilient systems and organisms that are best able to survive existential threats. During times of evolutionary transition, omnivores fare better than animals with specialized diets. Those who produce frequent and large litters outcompete those with fewer young and longer gestation periods. Those with adaptive traits like warm-bloodedness or parthenogenesis are much more likely to persevere through periods of environmental hardship.

The same is true for humans. We are one of the most adaptive species nature has ever created. And we are capable of greatness. We can be builders or destroyers. Stewards or spoilers. On the same acreage, we can choose to erect a strip mall or an organic farm. It all comes down to *choice*. We've been pursuing a course of de-generation. But it's just as much in our power to embrace re-generation instead.

The Kübler-Ross model mentioned earlier dials through Denial, Anger, Bargaining, Depression—finally ending at Acceptance. And we find that once people make their way to this stage, a whole new set of possibilities starts to open up. At this point, emotions swing away from fear and back to hope as realization sets in that we have an over-abundance of opportunity to do things differently, more intelligently, and more sustainably. We have the chance to look at everything afresh, challenge old assumptions, and make new choices—many of which, while potentially quite different from the ones we've made in the past, nurture us in ways we didn't realize we needed.

And so we return to the importance of narrative, and of the need for a new one that better serves us.

Two quotes from the great civil rights leader Mahatma Gandhi underscore the wisdom of cultivating useful narratives, whether at the individual or societal level. The first explains how our beliefs, which are shaped by the stories we tell ourselves, have a cascading impact on the reality we experience:

> *"Your beliefs become your thoughts,*
> *Your thoughts become your words,*
> *Your words become your actions,*
> *Your actions become your habits,*
> *Your habits become your values,*
> *Your values become your destiny."*

The clear logic of this progression provides a compelling reason for hope. If the path of our destiny is set in motion by the narrative we hold, then if we change the narrative, we can change our destiny.

Let's look at some of the main narratives our society holds right now:

- 3%+ GDP growth will rescue our economy. All efforts to make that happen are necessary, even if they punish the prudent.

- American energy independence is just around the corner.

- Our banks are too-big-to-fail (or jail) and therefore need to be supported at taxpayer cost.

- Enhancing national security requires sacrificing more of our civil liberties.

- Gold is not money.
- We're all better off if the stock market is higher.
- Most of our social problems (schools, jobs, global competitiveness, etc.) will be solved with more taxes and more regulation.
- Housing and education loans are "good debt."
- We live in a completely free and fair society.
- The Fed knows what it is doing.

Nearly all of these is either arbitrary, favoring of certain groups over others, self-destructive, or straight-up delusional.

What if we replaced them with the following ones instead?

- To leave a sustainable future for our progeny, nations must learn to live within their economic, energetic and ecological budgets.
- Humans can be incredible forces of regeneration, creating abundance wherever and whenever they wish.
- No one is above the rule of law. All laws should be applied equally regardless of class, race or any other demographic categorization.
- We are stewards, not exploiters, of the planet and its finite resources. Conservation trumps consumption, whenever possible.
- A nation's currency should be a means of exchange and a store of value—period. It's not to be manipulated for political reasons.
- Those entrusted with the most power are required to demonstrate the most proof behind the decisions they make.

Were we to embrace new stories like the above, how different would our priorities and actions be today? Vastly different, in our estimation. We would be investing orders of magnitude more into renewable energy sources and electrifying the transportation grid, and orders of magnitude less on fracked wells and SUV manufacturing. We would be treating our top-soils and fisheries as natural treasures, not as ATMs. Those caught trying to influence market prices would be in prison, not in the boardroom.

The point is: once the *narrative* changes, a whole new set of outcomes becomes possible.

The same is true at the individual level. Changing your personal narrative to align better with the future you wish to see frees you up from many of the ropes bound to you by your current one. It gives you permission to focus on developing the 8 Forms of Capital—to deepen other aspects of your life that society may even, in some cases, discourage you from attending to.

And most importantly, this world of alignment and opportunity gives you a positive view of the future to step into. No longer are you operating out of fear or doubt. The pit in your stomach warning you: *I really shouldn't to be living like this* is gone. Instead, hope, purpose and optimism bloom. Self-esteem returns. Regardless of what the future brings, you're now truly *living*.

In our work at Peak Prosperity, we see an abundance of inspirational examples of such progress demonstrated by many of the resiliency pioneers we talk with, as well as many of our readers who have undergone transformation in their lives.

We've personally seen the benefits a shift in personal narrative can bring. Both of us experienced sizable life changes when we left our corporate executive roles to pursue our mission, a big one being a dramatic drop in income. But we had worked in advance on re-defining what 'wealth' meant to us. True, money still plays a material role in our calculation of wealth, but we decided that there are many other components with an equal footing (purpose, health, self-sufficiency, strong relationships, time in nature, community involvement, etc.). We believed we could *cut our standard of living in half, yet double our quality of life.*

That was a foundational narrative for us. And it helped us weather the 'tight times' that ensued as we worked to get PeakProsperity.com off the ground. Holding that aspiration, along with a practical plan (with specific goals and milestones), really did take a lot of the worry and stress away during a time when, without it, we easily could have become consumed by the shock of the lost income and the uncertainty of our venture.

These are just a few examples of how embracing a narrative focused on resilience leads to empowering results. The better destiny it offers is there for the taking. But you've got to grasp it yourself.

Returning back to Gandhi in closing: another of his maxims is often paraphrased as "*Be the change you wish to see in the world.*" A wise sentiment from a wise man.

Such change only comes from within.

And starts with getting our stories straight.

CHAPTER 4

OBSTACLES TO SUCCESS

Your author Chris remembers the first time he went out to buy emergency storage food at the local grocery store. He loaded up his cart with beans, rice, sugar and other staples. Hat tucked low over his sunglasses, a roll of cash in his pocket; he repeatedly rehearsed a cover story in his head in case anyone asked him what the supplies were for. After all, it was a pretty ridiculous-looking cart of food.

He was nervous throughout: worried of judgment from the other shoppers or, god forbid, from someone who recognized him. His stomach was tied in knots just from the simple act of buying food with the intention of storing it long-term *just in case*. Nobody would understand, he feared, thinking it was too outside of the social norm in his area. It's just not something that normal people *do*.

That was back in 2004, over ten years ago. Of course today he'd have no problem saying what he was up to and why. But, sadly, shopping *just in case* is still socially different enough to raise a few eyebrows and make things slightly awkward.

Which brings us to the heart of this chapter: the obstacles that may prevent you from taking steps towards resilience.

Based on our experience, most people don't take any steps at all to secure a better future for themselves. And not because of any limitations in ability or resources; quite the opposite. Instead, it's the emotional intangibles like fear, limiting beliefs and social pressures that usually trip folks up, many of which have no rational basis.

We're going to spend some time deconstructing these now, because the more you understand them, the less power they will have over you.

SOCIAL PRESSURE

You might find yourself avoiding getting started down the path of becoming resilient simply because, as Chris experienced, it's socially awkward and uncomfortable.

Most people don't want to do anything too far out of social norms. And as hard as it is typically for most people to go against the social herd, with the material we cover it can be a pretty tall order. Preparing for disruptions to our modern lifestyle flies in the face of society's sense of "normal".

Most folks fear change, and they want to believe in the re-assuring dream —sold daily by our media and politicians—that everything's great, and is only going to get better with each passing year. If they see you taking steps that signal you may not believe 100% in that promise, they interpret it as a challenge—likely one triggered by an inner unspoken anxiety that if *they're* wrong, then they're really vulnerable. You may even get teased and ridiculed as a "doomer," "survivalist," or "tin-foil-hat prepper."

Not everyone is willing to sign up for that kind of social shaming, and as a result, most people won't prepare for crisis in advance.

State and federal government agencies tasked with emergency preparedness are well-acquainted with this dynamic, perhaps best illustrated by the fact that only a small minority of people living on active earthquake zones in California have even the most minimal of preparations stored away in their closets or garages.

This means that the vast majority of the people living on top of destructive faults have no water, no blankets, no hand crank operated radios, and no food set aside for the possibility, or we should say *eventuality*, of an earthquake. And this is despite active programs of education and cajoling by various state and federal agencies with hefty budgets aimed at getting people to prepare. As we said, it's not entirely rational.

A rational person would calculate the odds of an event, multiply it by its potential severity or catastrophic potential, and then calculate the amount of effort and money they'd be willing to spend to protect themselves and their family.

So in the case of people living on top of the San Andreas fault, the calculation might be (an unacceptably high probability) x (a catastrophic outcome) = (*I should really do something!*).

What would "doing something" actually cost? Not very much. To locate and purchase a 72-hour emergency kit for a family of four would require perhaps ten minutes online and $50 for a basic version (the deluxe version is roughly $150). Many people spend more money than this on coffee each month, and far more time on the Internet watching cat videos. So it's not really the cost, in terms of time or money, which prevents them from taking action.

What explains it then? What prevents people from even taking minimal, prudent actions that could literally make the difference between life and death? If it's not a rational calculation, then what is it?

Fortunately psychology helps us to understand what's really at play. Social pressure it is definitely a big inhibitor to action, but we have to go a bit deeper to understand the rest.

PAIN AND INSIGHT

If you're a dentist you'll be quite familiar with this next part.

Most people resist change and tend to avoid anything that's uncomfortable. These are not usually wise strategies, and they often backfire, but this is how most humans react. We remain in our comfort zone until forced out of it. The more uncomfortable the threat, the greater our willful denial. People easily ignore uncomfortable truths—bad health habits, mounting unpaid bills, declining 401k statements—even though the repercussions of this negligence can have a material and detrimental impact on the rest of their lives.

However, life rolls on and we cannot ignore everything forever, especially things with inevitable consequences. Sooner or later we have to either decide to change our behavior, on our own terms, or else run smack into reality's hard limits. Said another way, there are two ways that people decide to change: by insight, and by pain.

It's only after the heart attack, the divorce, the backing over the family dog while drunk—moments of extreme pain—that most people will begin to actively face the idea that they need to make different decisions in life. Change by the pain route is something that we all do now and then in life. It's simply part of the deal and it's very common.

But it doesn't have to be the whole deal. Part of the beauty of being human is that we can learn from observation, reflection and experience, and can adapt. Someone buying a 72-hour emergency kit *before* the next earthquake strikes is acting via insight.

We wrote this book to help you make your life changes now, via insight. Hopefully, that's why you picked it up.

The story told by the Three Es is loaded with the potential for plenty of painful moments over the next few decades. Sadly, a lot of people will not take precautionary steps far enough in advance to matter. They're just not focusing on the risks right now. As a result, much of the world will be forced to change its behavior via the pain route.

Use this awareness as a sense of urgency to prepare now. To secure your future prosperity, as well as to help those regretting that they didn't follow your lead.

THE COMMON REASONS 'WHY NOT'

In our conversations with thousands of folks through our website and seminars, here are the most frequent excuses we hear for avoiding taking action today:

- **Social Shame** – My family and friends will think I'm 'crazy'. (this is another way of saying *"I don't want to commit social suicide."*)

- **Lack of Awareness** – If I'm not familiar with these risks and if they're not immediately apparent when I look out my front door, then maybe they're not real. (This is the *"Ignorance is bliss"* defense.)

- **Too Uncomfortable** – I don't like thinking about things that make me uncomfortable. (This is the *"Don't ruin my vibe"* mindset.)

- **Too Limited** – I don't have the time/money/etc. to focus on this right now. (This is the *"Hey, I have a life, in case you hadn't noticed"* pushback.)

- **Too Superstitious** – If I give voice to my worries, then they're more likely to occur. (This is the *"He-who-must-not-be-named"* defense.)

- **Too Scary** – I don't want to live in fear. (This is the *"Dear God, we're all gonna die!"* rebuke.)

- **Not a Problem #1** – Humans are clever. Somebody smart will invent a solution in time. (This *"faith in technology"* meme is very prevalent in today's culture.)

- **Not a Problem #2** – "They" will never let that happen. (This *"faith in authority"* is a close second behind technology.)

- **Not Credible** – Well, I haven't heard it from NBC News/ Oprah/my dad/[insert other trusted source here] yet, so how big a deal could this be? (This is the *"Who the heck are you?"* rebuttal.)

There's one thing every one of these "reasons" share in common. Each is the product of a *belief system*.

In the previous chapter, we discussed the powerful influence of narrative and beliefs. Beliefs may be of either the enhancing form (*I'm lucky!*) or of the limiting variety (*I'm unlucky!*). Beliefs operate on an unconscious level although they play out in our lives every day in very real ways. They are immensely potent in shaping our decisions, far more than is commonly realized.

> *"Until you make the unconscious conscious, it will direct your life and you will call it fate."*
>
> —Carl Jung

Holding even one of the above beliefs (let alone several in combination) can be sufficient to stop any potential action dead it in its tracks.

At Peak Prosperity we spend a good deal of time understanding and helping people shift beliefs. Until and unless a blocking belief is removed or minimized, action is usually stymied.

SHIFTING YOUR BELIEFS

So how can you shift a limiting belief into an enhancing one?

Beliefs are something that we hold to be true and seem to be supported by daily experience and facts. While we may intuitively consider them to be entrenched and immovable elements of our psyches, we actually shift them all the time—raise your hand if you still believe in the Tooth Fairy, the Easter bunny, fairies, or Santa Claus?

Once new information comes along, beliefs can shift. But first there's an emotional unhooking process that has to run.

Here's how we know when we're debating someone who is operating from a belief system rather than simply holding an opinion. The more we argue, the more emotional they become. Facts don't matter. The more facts that run up against this person's beliefs, the angrier or sadder or volatile they become.

This is because our beliefs are hooked up to our deepest selves. They are wired right into our amygdala and bypass our rational brain centers.

On the other hand, a person holding an *opinion* can shift that opinion relatively easily if presented with new data.

Suppose you're shopping for a new vacuum cleaner. You've gathered the product specs, read the reviews and have formed an opinion about which one is best for your needs. Then along comes a friend who has new first-hand information with that model that causes you to change your mind.

Does this shift in opinion get you riled up? No, of course not. It's just an opinion.

Not so with beliefs. Shifting those takes emotional energy, sometimes a lot of it. It takes time and courage to consciously examine and alter our deeply-held beliefs. Not very many people do this or are even willing to try.

In her research into the grieving process which we touched on in the previous chapter, Elizabeth Kubler-Ross talked about this exact dynamic when we are confronted by the most belief-challenging experience of them all: our own death. When our own mortality finally breathes down on us, we tend to go through a very predictable set of *emotional* responses: denial, anger, bargaining, depression and acceptance.

These five stages of grief play out virtually every time a belief system is challenged. The more entrenched the belief, the stronger the emotional resistance to changing it. But regardless of whether the belief is tiny or large, confronting our beliefs is always an emotional process.

We might feel that we have to give up something cherished, which feels like a loss to us. Perhaps it's faith in authority that we may have to relinquish, or the hope that our children will have as many opportunities as we did, or that technology will ride to the rescue in time.

The main reason people avoid developing resilience is because doing so usually asks them to confront one or more closely held-beliefs and is therefore an invitation to a certain amount of emotional stress.

Another thing about beliefs is that they are incredibly good at harvesting data that supports their continuation and solidification, and are amazingly good at either rejecting or completely overlooking data that would undermine them. This is obviously at play with climate change, where various camps cherry pick their data to support their case while ignoring mountains of evidence that would refute their positions.

So let's look at some of the common excuses again and see if we can identify the beliefs at play:

Social Shame – *My family and friends will think I'm 'crazy.'*

Our social conditioning has led us to believe that bad things will befall us if we are seen in a poor light by the people around us, as illustrated by Chris' bulk food shopping adventure.

The belief in play is that it's wrong somehow to deviate from social convention. The repercussions can hurt: a loss of social standing, shunning, and damaged relationships, which then translate into the loss of love and connection. So being seen as crazy or nuts is really a threat to our ability to feel loved and be connected, which means it's wired right into one of the most emotionally-charged areas of our psyches.

When we find ourselves disguising our actions it indicates that shame is the emotion in charge. Shame is a very powerful method of social control, used in the socialization process, which gets internalized at an early age.

It keeps us in line, but does it really serve us? What if we could reduce or eliminate unnecessary shame? Would our social lives and connections improve or degrade? It's interesting to note that culturally we admire and idolize the rebels and (seemingly) shameless celebrities. The wilder and more confident the better.

What would happen if we simply openly acted in accordance with our inner guidance and accumulated wisdom? Honestly, it's more probable that people would admire and follow us than ridicule and shun us.

> *Lack of Awareness – If I'm not familiar with these risks and if they're not immediately apparent when I look out my front door, then maybe they're not real.*

This one is denial, plain and simple. It's the most common stage we encounter. It plays an important role as the gatekeeper that actively prevents the rest of the emotional sequence from being triggered. Denial is a self-defense mechanism that allows us to avoid looking at things so that we don't have to open an entire can of worms.

Sometimes this is actually a legitimate and useful strategy. For the person who is otherwise unable to cope with more emotional stimulation at the time, perhaps a struggling single parent at the end of their reserves, or someone battling a serious health crisis, choosing battles carefully is a wise move.

But for most others, denial is a poor strategy because it makes us more vulnerable to the risks we close our eyes to.

> *Too Limited – I don't have the time/money/etc to focus on this right now.*

This belief is a common one, which we run into all the time. At its core is a limiting belief that one does not have the resources to get the job done well. And this regularly leads to *nothing* getting done, even though everyone has the resources to get *something* done.

The person holding this belief might have deep-seated fears of failure or losing what they have. The underlying beliefs manifest in feelings of powerlessness and insufficiency.

However, we know people of extremely limited means who have made huge strides in preparedness using practically no money. One, a divorced mother of four, with no savings to speak of, became highly prepared entirely on a shoestring budget. She prioritized her time, was scrappy, made excellent use of online swap and classified sites, and took advantage of the fact that if you live in America, you live around a lot of people with more stuff than they want or know what to do with.

The point here is that everyone has capacity to prioritize toward preparing, but they first have to elevate the priority above other commitments. The statement that *I have no time, money or resources* is a pure limiting belief. If you hold it, those things may as well be true.

By identifying our limiting beliefs, we can expose them for the frauds they are and begin the process of removing them from our lives and replacing them with enhancing beliefs. As Gandhi said, *our beliefs shape our destiny*. Rather than being captive to our beliefs, we can consciously choose them!

And finally:

> *Not a Problem #1 – Humans are clever. Somebody smart will invent a solution in time.*

This is faith in technology and it's a doozy. For all of our lives, technology has only been getting more elaborate and more powerful. And while it's certainly true that technology will continue to get better at the things it does, we shouldn't let our faith in it cause us to overlook the things it *cannot* do.

Technology is only as good as the people using it. For instance, GPS is wonderful. It enables us to easily and safely navigate the trickiest of cities effortlessly. But it also allows gigantic fishing trawlers to drop their massive weighted nets six inches to the left of where they left off last week, ensuring that the ocean bottom is thoroughly scraped. As a result, many of the largest commercial fishing grounds, like the once-massive Northern cod fishery in the Grand Banks, have collapsed. That is, our cultural decision-making has not evolved as fast as the technology. Think 'monkeys with machine guns' and you're on the right track.

Technology also cannot create energy. It can find it, use it more efficiently and help us do far more with less, but it cannot *create* energy. If our faith in technology causes us to overlook the risks of fossil fuels on and in our lives then that belief system will bite us. Why? Because fossil fuels are *the* source of energy that provide our food, our warmth, our lights and our fuel. Technology does not create energy, it *uses* energy. Technology alone cannot create new deposits fossil fuels for us, even if we wanted it to. Instead we should be eyes-wide-open about what technology can and cannot do, and plan our lives accordingly.

FROM BELIEF TO ACTION

The path to shifting beliefs begins with identifying them. One sure-fire way to know you have a belief system at play is to note when your emotional defense mechanisms get activated.

Perhaps you get angry at someone's arguments, or you find yourself tuning out. Or do you find yourself ecstatically agreeing? Whenever you notice a charge or resistance concerning an idea, it means that there's an emotion-based belief governing your thinking in that area.

Sometimes all that's necessary to begin shifting a belief is simply becoming aware that it exists in the first place. Your emotional reactions to things are your best clues.

Once you've found a thread to follow, the next step is to see if you can isolate it. Where did it come from? How long has it been with you? What's actually at the core of it?

These are not simple or one-and-done sorts of inquiries. Discovering your operating beliefs is more of a spiral process where with each pass around you learn a little bit more, gain a bit more insight, and dig a bit deeper.

But beliefs can be shifted and the better you get at it the better your life will become.

To paraphrase Gandhi, with the right mindset, anything is possible.

Now that you know which beliefs to embrace and which to avoid, it's time to focus on developing your resilience action plan.

CHAPTER 5

OK... SO HOW DO I DEVELOP RESILIENCE?

Resilience lives in the overlap of having the right mindset and performing the right actions, at the intersection of "knowing" and "doing":

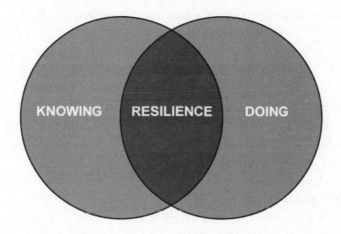

We've spent the chapters of this book so far working on the "knowing" part. By now, you should have a clear understanding of the major trends mostly likely to shape our way of life over the next several decades. And you should also have an appreciation of the types of constructive narratives that we should be guiding ourselves by, as a society and as individuals, if we want to avoid collapse and instead create a future worth inheriting.

The rest of this book will focus on the "actions" side of the equation. We'll lay out the specific solution sets that we've come to learn, though our years of study and personal implementation, are the most essential and effective for advancing one's resilience.

If you indeed put these actions into practice, you will be substantially better positioned to persevere through adversity—whether that be a natural disaster, the sudden loss of income or a loved one, a meltdown of the financial system, or a slow downwards grind in living standards as energy becomes more expensive.

Even if our trend forecasts turn out to be *completely* erroneous—you will still win! Not only will you have dodged the 'living in crisis' bullet, but you'll be healthier, happier, more socially connected, and wealthier because of these actions. When you think about it that way, it's pretty crazy that everybody isn't already onboard the resilience train.

STARTING RIGHT

As we begin, there are a few foundational perspectives to keep in mind.

Remember that resilience is a journey, not a destination. Just as with learning in life, there is no point at which you're "done." You will never be 100% prepared for every possible scenario, so don't put that pressure on yourself. The goal is *steady improvement*—a little bit of progress at a time. As with a long journey, each small step may feel insufficient on its own—but each one is *necessary*.

Start with the areas that need the most attention, and once you've shored them up to a higher standard, switch your focus to others areas before cycling back again. Then repeat, repeat, repeat…

You'll find after time that your efforts will gradually shift from reducing your vulnerabilities to enhancing your capabilities. This is the point at which you'll truly begin to understand that resilience is all about creating a better tomorrow versus defending against the loss of what we have today. Be warned, though: this is when the process begins to get pretty addictive.

The 'lone wolf' is a myth . When some people hear the word "resilience", they think "survivalist." This conjures up visions of fully self-sufficient bunkers hidden in the wilderness, chock full of MREs and ammo—truly a "me-against-the-world" stance. To be crystal clear, this is NOT the approach we advocate.

First off, it's the rare individual—as in, less than 1% of the population rare—who actually has the constitution and the mindset to live this way. The rest of us would fail or self-eject from that life for a critical reason: *we need others*. Humans are social creatures and, yes, our emotional health diminishes without community interaction. Further, we can't be experts in everything, and so we need to rely on those whose complementary expertise and assets shore up our own deficiencies.

Plus, who *wants* to cower in an isolated bunker in the woods? What kind of existence is that??

Remember that developing resilience is a *selfless* act, not a selfish act. We sometimes find that people feel uncomfortable focusing so much on their own situation. *What about the needs of others?* they ask. Our short answer is that improving your own state of resilience is one of the best things you can do to be in service to those around you.

How?

Well, should hardship arrive, you won't be one of the unprepared needing assistance and support. So right off the bat, you're not demanding precious resources in a time of crisis. More than that, you'll likely be able to be an asset to your community during this time: providing care, or contributing some of your own surplus supplies to those who didn't plan ahead as you did. We strongly believe that given the same stresses, some communities will fare better than others—with the difference between them being driven, in part, by the level of resilience of their respective populations. If having a resilient community is important to you, the most important step you can take is getting your own house in order.

Time is your greatest asset. So start now. Right now, as of the writing of this book, everything still works. Fossil energy is cheap relative to the work it can do for us, and still widely available. The economy is not in recession (at least, not officially). The stores are well-stocked. This is the time—when things are abundant, affordable and tranquil—to be investing in your preparation for a future shaped by the Three Es.

If you wait, you risk waiting too long. Once crisis arrives, not only will it be much harder and more expensive to acquire the preparations you need—they may not be available at any price. And your efforts to procure them will no longer be prudent planning—instead, they'll be a means of hoarding, pitting you against desperate others in your community.

An example: on March 11, 2011, a 10-dose packet of potassium iodide pills (a first line of defense against nuclear contamination) could be purchased for $12 at any number of U.S. retailers. One day later, within hours after the first hydrogen explosion at Japan's Fukushima Daiichi nuclear facility, the entire supply of potassium iodide pills within America was sold out. The outage lasted nearly three months, during which the pills could not be found on the open market at any price.

STEP ZERO

Many people, when daunted by the potential magnitude of the coming change, immediately jump to some very hard conclusions that prove incapacitating. For example, they may have thoughts such as, *I need to go back to school to get an entirely different degree so I can have a different job!* or *I need to completely relocate to a new area and start over, leaving all my friends behind!* These panic-driven conclusions may feel so radical that they're quickly abandoned. As a result, nothing gets accomplished. Further, nearly everyone has hidden barriers to action lurking within.

Our advice here is crisp and clear. Find the smallest and easiest thing you can do, and then do it. We don't care what it is. If that thing for you is buying an extra jar of pimentos because you can't imagine life without them, then buy an extra jar next time you're shopping and put it in the pantry. We're only *slightly* joking here.

We call this **Step Zero** to symbolize something minor that might precede step one.

The point is that small steps lead to bigger steps. If you have not yet taken *step one* toward personal preparation and resilience, we invite you to consider taking *step zero*.

Examples might be taking out a small bit of extra cash to store outside of the bank in case of a banking disruption, buying a bit more food each week that can slowly deepen your pantry, or going online to learn something more about ways you can increase your resilience with regard to water, food, energy, or anything else you deem important to your future. It doesn't so much matter what it is, as long as an action is taken.

Don't forget: There was a time when each of us took our own Step Zeroes.

For Chris, as he described in the previous chapter, it was buying extra food. He felt so awkward and self-conscious while doing it that he considered driving to a grocery store several towns away where there would be less of a chance of someone recognizing him overloading his cart.

For Adam, it was buying his first ounces of gold. He agonized about how to make the purchase, eventually deciding to buy bullion through Australia's Perth Mint, which would also store the gold. After a little while, he got uncomfortable with the gold being held overseas, and paid to have Brinks deliver it to him in the States. After that, he got nervous holding it himself at home, so then bounced it around among a few private storage facilities until he finally concluded he was just over-thinking things way too much. In the end these first ounces of gold may be among the most well traveled in human history.

So, if you feel a little hesitant about taking that first step, perhaps embarrassed to do something that's a little socially "not-normal," you're not alone. We've been there. It gets easier as you take more steps. The awkwardness goes away, replaced by a growing peace of mind that you're finally taking a degree of control over your destiny.

And as for the social insecurities, our experience is that *no one really cares*. In many cases, those who actually notice and ask questions usually find what you're doing novel and intriguing. In fact, it often opens up a conversation about the Three Es that they wouldn't have felt socially comfortable bringing up in other situations, like a cocktail party or soccer game.

So, what's your Step Zero going to be?

STAGES OF RESILIENCE

Now, not everyone reading this is at the same stage when it comes to resilience. Some of you have yet to take Step Zero; others of you may already be years into the process.

From our work with thousands of people over the past decade, we've observed that people generally fall into one of three "stages" of resilience. It's helpful to identify which one you fall into, and what you need to attend to in order to be ready (if interested) to advance to the next stage.

Stage One

This is where the vast majority of the folks we encounter land. Many have yet to take Step Zero, or otherwise still have a high degree of exposure to the Three Es. Their primary goals are safety and security, often with an urgent focus on protecting their financial wealth.

Fear can be a big driver for those in Stage One. They fear losing the assets they've worked hard in life to accumulate, and they fear the physical dangers that times of struggle may bring to themselves and their loved ones. They may also dread the loss of our modern standard of living. As a result, they tend to be more reactive than proactive, attending to whichever stressor is aggrieving them most at any given moment.

Given their low level of resilience, those in Stage One are best served by working to develop basic readiness across the essential areas of resilience. Since money is of major concern, re-allocating their financial capital towards safety is a usual first step. Food and water storage, emergency preparedness, home security, and the basics of community development are other areas of primary focus.

These folks tend to feel overwhelmed by the brain-stretching ramifications of the risks outlined in *The Crash Course*. Combined with the fears we've mentioned, a deer-in-headlights immobility is common. No surprise, many in Stage One ask for handheld, by-the-numbers guidance; which was a big motivator in writing this book. The following chapters, and the accompanying *What Should I Do?* guide in particular, were intentionally created to provide crisp, specific guidance.

Stage Two

Those in Stage Two tend to have a much more positive and optimistic outlook. They've achieved a foundational level of resilience across all essential areas, and as a result, their feelings of immediate and acute vulnerability have greatly diminished, replaced by a growing peace of mind as they continue deepening their preparedness for *whatever* the future may bring.

With the defense-oriented basics already taken care of, Stage Two residents spend most of their efforts instead on advancing their capabilities. Food and energy production, skill development, career transition, community involvement, therapy—all are examples of the areas focused on more during Stage Two. (The accompanying workbook provides a lot of specific direction for those in this stage, too.)

By acquiring these new abilities and roles, folks increasingly realize that freeing themselves from the old narrative and norms opens up rich new opportunities for re-invention and self-betterment. And this just makes them increasingly excited to progress faster. It's a chance to start over, to do things more "right," and to live with greater purpose and quality of life. Many describe this stage as "becoming more of the person they had always intended to be."

Stage Three

Heartened by the personal growth experienced in Stage Two, those in Stage Three live in accordance with the Peak Prosperity mission of "creating a world worth inheriting." They're rich where it counts in terms of investment in resilience, and their focus is now turned outwards, towards helping others develop the same mastery and self-actualized life they have.

They seek to share their knowledge and to create resources future generations will benefit from. Civic involvement, community leadership, education, mentoring, legacy investing, and business formation are examples of activities those in Stage Three engage in.

Self-Assessment

Many of you reading this probably have a good sense of which Stage you currently fall into. But specifically: where are you secure, and where are your vulnerabilities? What kind of future are you hoping for? What steps are most important to start taking today in order to successfully position yourself for it? Do you have the resources you'll need?

Having an honest and accurate appraisal of where you are today, your strengths as well as your deficiencies, will be necessary for developing your resilience plan.

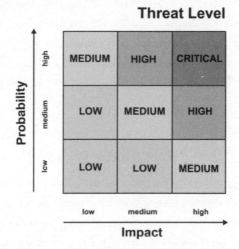

We've developed a free self-assessment form for you to use for exactly this purpose. You can access it at http://www.peakprosperity.com/selfassessment.

Download it and fill it out when you have time to give it your full attention. The subsequent steps you take in your resilience-building will be based in large part on your answers to this document.

THE JOURNEY IS NON-LINEAR

Another good thing to keep in mind about the process of building resilience is that it's non-linear. You don't move from Point A to Point B, etc., until one day you're at the finish line.

Instead, you do what you can in the moment, move on, and then return again and again to each area of preparation, re-evaluating and iterating.

The Japanese have a term for this: *kaizen*. Literally translated as "change for better," *kaizen* refers to the practice of continuous improvement. It has been used to great success in manufacturing, and is credited with Japan's amazing economic recovery following the devastation of the Second World War.

Under *kaizen*, a process is run, measured, evaluated, and then optimized. Once this progression has happened, it's repeated. And repeated. And so on. With every repeat of the cycle, the process gets better.

You should view your resilience-building efforts similarly. Don't expect to get to perfect—in anything. It's just not practical, nor is it realistic. Just concentrate on getting a little bit better each time.

THE VALUE OF MISTAKES

Another reason the *kaizen* framework is useful to know about is that it bears strikingly similar resemblance to the way in which our minds learn.

To gain new knowledge—to become smarter—our brain formulates a hypothesis, tests it out, observes the results, processes them, and then begins the cycle anew:

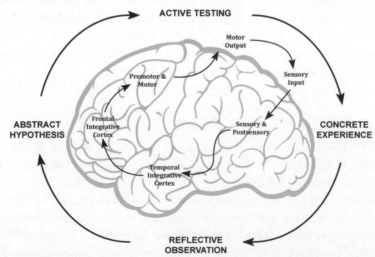

This test-and-measure, or "trial-and-error" approach is the way we are wired for self-betterment, which brings us to the importance of mistakes.

When building resilience, you're going to make them. A *lot* of them. You'll be trying things you've never done before, across all aspects of your life. And much of the coming change on a macro level is out of your control, making it impossible to predict without error. Mistakes are inevitable.

This scares many. Some to the point of immobility. You need to get past that fear.

Why?

Well, as we've hopefully just demonstrated, mistakes are required for learning and self-development. Whether it's manufacturing a Toyota or growing a tomato, our brains need to observe an outcome and then ask: *What could we change to do it better next time?* We need to experience how it doesn't work perfectly in order to imagine how it might in the future.

During his long path to eventual success in inventing a long-lasting electric light bulb, inventor Thomas Edison famously quipped: *I haven't failed. I've just found 10,000 ways that won't work.*

When we fail, we need to conjure our inner Edison to remind us that the only true failure lies in failing to try. We must remember that the goofs, the glitches, the curve balls—the mistakes—are our milestones to mastery.

Mistakes are so important, in fact, that if you're not making them now, and plenty of them, you're putting yourself at a real disadvantage. Why? Because, as of the writing of this book, life still works pretty much as we've known it. Things are relatively tranquil in the world. This is the time to be making your mistakes—while the cost of failure is low, as is the threat level to your quality of life.

You know when's a terrible time to learn about how to put hedging safeguards into your financial portfolio? After the market has already corrected by 50% (as it last did during the 2008 crisis). Try figuring out how to source a meaningful percentage of your calories locally after a liquid fuels emergency has stopped the trucks delivering produce to your grocery market. Failure at that moment could be life-threatening.

So as you begin trying things you've never done before while working on your resilience, embrace the mistakes. Hope to make them, even.

Just make sure you learn from them.

"Mistakes are great, the more I make, the smarter I get."
—R. Buckminster Fuller

REMEMBER THE IMPORTANCE OF MINDSET

Helmuth von Multke the Elder was a German Field Marshall and military science innovator who led the Prussian Army for thirty years. Strategies he developed continue to influence warfare to this day. Suffice it to say, this guy had a lot of experience when it came to battles.

Given that depth of expertise, we should heed his famous declaration: *No battle plan ever survives first contact with the enemy.*

Or for those who prefer more modern references, let's take the words of the great American thinker, boxer Mike Tyson, when he similarly opined: *Everybody has a plan until they get punched in the mouth.*

What both of these august gentlemen are talking about is the reality in life that things rarely ever go according to your expectations.

With the combination of arriving macro risks and the inevitability of making a lot of mistakes in your personal preparations, a key success/ survival factor is going to be the strength of your constitution. Will you persevere through adversity? Or be crushed by it?

Here we find that the mindset of the entrepreneur is especially well-suited to thrive under such conditions of uncertainty, challenge and change. We've spent substantial time across several countries with Robert Kiyosaki, serial business owner and famed author of the *Rich Dad Poor Dad* series of books on entrepreneurship. In our discussions with him, we've noted his special appreciation for the following specific traits in the people he chooses to work with. They:

- Create value
- Identify opportunity
- Bounce back quickly from adversity
- Give their ALL at all times
- Learn from failure

We'll elaborate more on these traits in the coming chapter on Knowledge Capital, but it's worth flagging them now. No matter what your profession— corporate, medical, academic, government, agriculture, legal, artistic— these are traits to cultivate that will help you in both the here and now as well as the future to come.

GETTING STARTED

OK—enough context. Now it's time to roll up your sleeves and start doing.

The remainder of this book will focus on the 8 Forms of Capital, which are the building blocks for a resilient life:

8 FORMS OF CAPITAL

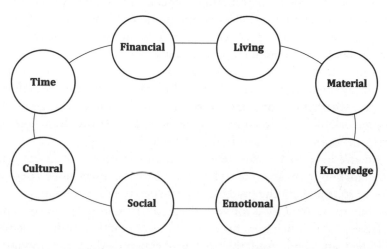

Again, the process of becoming resilient is going to take time, and you'll never be truly "done." It may be messy—hopefully you're going to make a lot of mistakes, and you may not find many people at the next cocktail party who understand why you're taking these steps.

But you're also taking control of your destiny and bringing your actions into alignment with what you believe to be true. That feels fantastic. And the more you prepare, the more peace of mind and confidence you will enjoy. Before long you will realize that you're able to do more, to be more, than you previously thought possible. You may even stop worrying about the Three E changes headed our way, and start becoming excited to step into a more authentic and sustainable way of living.

We say this from experience. We've taken many of these steps in our lives already, so we have an informed sense of what actions work and which ones don't. Our advice is not theory; it's based on what we've learned through our own practical application, or through the readers at PeakProsperity.com who have shared their learnings with us.

And when we started out, leaving the "safe" path our careers had been on, neither of us had the benefit of a guide like the one you're currently holding in your hands or knowing people who had safely jumped ship and made better lives for themselves. So if we could offer a word of encouragement it would be to not worry about the things you don't yet know or the skills you don't yet have, it's all going to work out fine for you.

You just need to roll up your sleeves and get started.

OUR ASK OF YOU

As we've been repeatedly hammering home, becoming more resilient takes time. So as you read the following chapters, challenge yourself to start putting the material into practice as soon as possible—as in, don't wait to finish the book before taking your first steps.

Having a sense of time urgency and remaining disciplined enough to make steady progress, no matter how slight, are two critical factors that will determine whether or not you're going to be successful in your goals.

So, our ask of you is to commit to devoting at least **one hour per week** over the next three months to resilience building.

It doesn't have to be an intense hour. But it needs to be consistent. Enough for you to make some real progress over the three-month period, as well as to start making the practice of resilience-building a habit.

Go buy some extra food for your deep pantry. Go for a run to improve your fitness. Invite a neighbor over for coffee to strengthen your community. Small steps are good. And they make it easier to then start taking the bigger ones.

But commit to a minimum of an hour per week. Before long, you'll likely find you're devoting much more time than that, out of the sheer pleasure of it.

And with that, let's dive into the 8 Forms of Capital.

CHAPTER 6

FINANCIAL CAPITAL

When we speak publicly about the Three E trends, most people who come up to us afterwards ask: *What should I do?* What we've learned is that most of them are really asking: *What should I do with my money???*

We get it. Most of us spend the majority of our waking hours at work, earning money that we hope will provide a secure future for ourselves and those we care about. The idea of losing our hard-won financial savings suddenly during another economic crisis, through job loss or a market crash, is a near-universal fear.

Given this sensitivity and the related urgency many have around it, we'll begin our journey in resilience-building by focusing on developing Financial Capital.

So how can we protect our money and its purchasing power? And how may we be able to use our insights of future trends to make more of it?

MONEY ≠ RESILIENCE

But first, let's get some perspective. It's very important to note that even though we're starting with Financial Capital, that does not mean it's more important to developing resilience than any of the seven other forms. It's not.

And let's be really clear about this. If all you have is Financial Capital, even if you have millions to your name, you are NOT resilient.

We'll explain why more fully as we dial through the other forms of capital in future chapters, but for now, suffice it to say that some of the least resilient people we encounter in our consulting work have 8-figure bank accounts or higher. This is due in part to how completely these folks have let their identity become defined by the size of their savings account. They live in fear of their money disappearing; afraid they'll have no purpose or worth in the world without it.

Don't get us wrong, though. Financial Capital is important: *it is often the easiest means by which you can acquire other forms of capital.*

Think about it. You don't use your dollars (or Euros, or Pounds, or Yen, etc) for a physical purpose. You don't build a house out of them. Eating them doesn't nourish you. Instead, you exchange them for goods and services that can.

SOME PEOPLE ARE SO POOR, ALL THEY HAVE IS MONEY

And this exchange not only leaves you with a desired asset. It can also leave you with a tremendous surplus of *Time* (one of the other forms of capital), as you didn't have to invest the labor to produce the acquired asset. Anyone who's ever built a house, grown a crop, or gone through medical school themselves has a real appreciation for the true time savings that exchanging money for goods and services offers.

Which is why we encourage you to start thinking more broadly about what "wealth" is. Yes, money is a very real part of wealth, but only a part. In addition to the cash to your name, are you healthy? Happy? Safe? Wise? Valued by others? Self-sufficient? Those are the real "assets" you truly want to end up with in life. Money is simply one of the means of acquiring things in life that we need or value.

If there's one light bulb we're trying to turn on in your head in this chapter, it's this: Think about your financial holdings as divided into two buckets.

The first bucket is your **Resilience-Building Fund**. This is the allotment you plan to exchange for other forms of capital in the near term.

The second is your **Financial Future Portfolio**. This is the money you will save and invest today, with the intent to exchange it for other forms of capital at a later time (i.e. years) in the future.

How much of your holdings should go into the seed fund? And what should you do with the money left in your financial portfolio?

We'll go into answering these questions in detail in this chapter. But first, it helps to start this journey with a clear picture of your current financial situation. After all, you can't make good decisions without good data.

THE FUNDAMENTALS OF YOUR MONEY

Given the enormous range of bright and well-educated people we interact with each month at PeakProsperity.com, we're constantly surprised by the education gap many of them live with in regards to their personal finances.

Money is a topic often burdened by a lot of emotion for many people. As behavioral economist Dan Ariely has empirically cataloged in his book, *Predictably Irrational,* we humans frequently make inefficient, even nonsensical decisions around money – despite it being extremely quantifiable and trackable. For a number of fascinating cognitive reasons, bias, avarice and fear color our judgment in many ways of which we are usually unaware. The result? We often avoid the topic completely, or make hasty reactions to short-term issues—both of which undermine good decision-making.

Which is why your first steps towards Financial Resiliency start with taking a hard, honest look at your current situation. How much in savings do you have, after subtracting any debts you owe? Are you living within your means when it comes to your monthly income and expenses?

If you don't have the data readily at hand to answer these questions, don't worry. In the *What Should I Do?* workbook that accompanies this book, we have helpful templates and step-by-step guidance that makes the process of putting together your personal financial picture easy.

> **LISTEN:**
>
> 🎙
>
> *Dan Airely Podcast*
>
> **TOPIC:**
> *Behavioral Economics*
>
> **URL and LINK:**
> *See page 205*

While everyone's financial situation is unique, having this insight allows you to start crafting informed responses to important questions like:

- Do I have enough net wealth to fund my life's goals? If not, how much more do I need?

- Am I too indebted for comfort?

- Should I prioritize increasing my assets, or paying down my debts?

- Are my financial assets well-diversified?

- Are there any assets I'd prefer to sell now versus holding longer?
- Which debts should I pay off first?

DIVIDING YOUR BUCKETS

Armed with this new-found clarity into your finances, it's now time to make an important decision: *How much money are you going to allocate to your Resilience-Building Fund?*

Don't worry about being "exactly right" at this moment. You'll refine your answer as you go through the rest of this book and the exercises in the accompanying workbook. But it's important at this time to make a ballpark commitment of how much of your Financial Capital you're willing and able to start exchanging in return for other forms of capital that you may be currently deficient in.

Why now?

Well, first, this is your initial step towards making the mind-shift away from thinking about 'wealth' strictly in financial terms. And, secondly, the money that remains comprises your Financial Future Portfolio. The rest of this chapter will focus on how to increase both the size of your Financial Future Portfolio as well as its ability to weather unexpected shocks.

As with all things financial, how much you decide to devote at this point to your Resilience-Building Fund is a personal decision unique to your own situation and goals. But as a general benchmark, we recommend a starting range of between 10-15%. We'll give plenty of guidance on how to consider best allocating this in the upcoming chapters.

And for the money that remains in your Financial Future Portfolio, you must take care to ensure it's managed well. The many worrisome trends summarized in Chapter 2 and by *The Crash Course* practically guarantee that the future will see a higher degree of price volatility in the financial markets, economic crises, currency devaluations, relapses into recession, tax increases, and job market weakness. An investment portfolio managed in the old paradigm of buy-and-hold, "set-it-and-forget-it" has a dangerously elevated risk of being ravaged in this new environment.

START BY SAFEGUARDING

"*Primum non nocere*" ("First, do no harm") is a founding principle of bioethics that all healthcare students are taught. When it comes to managing your Future Financial Portfolio, we feel a similar commitment to safety and loss-avoidance is wise to adopt.

For this reason, we recommend that you strongly consider working under the guidance of a seasoned financial adviser, one who understands and appreciates the outlook and risks presented in *The Crash Course*, and who excels at risk-management. On our own, most of us lack the knowledge and the ability to hedge our investment positions effectively and affordably. And with busy lives, nearly all of us lack the time that active portfolio management will require in the high-volatility era we're entering. A responsible, prudent, experienced financial adviser can provide valuable stewardship here—though you do need to do your due diligence to find one of quality.

First and foremost, only consider advisers who convince you they truly understand your unique situation, goals and needs—and are willing to build a personalized investment strategy around them. A good sign you're dealing with the right kind of adviser is if they demonstrate a high listening-to-speaking ratio and take the time to ask clarifying questions.

There are far too many wealth management 'professionals' out there who only care about getting their hands on your hard-earned savings, which they will then toss into a one-size-fits-all portfolio that maximizes their earned fees and minimizes the time they need to spend managing it. We've been shocked by the many stories folks have shared with us about abysmal neglect their portfolios have suffered under such advisers; and a good number of these accounts had balances in the millions, leading us to wonder: *How huge does an account need to be to qualify for active oversight?*

As mentioned earlier, we strongly urge you to select an advisor with demonstrated years of risk-management experience. By this, we mean using investment allocations and instruments that provide downside protection to your portfolio, in case the market moves against you—a practice frequently referred to as 'hedging.' Hedging can be as simple as holding a higher percentage of your portfolio in cash when markets seem dangerously 'frothy,' but it can get quite complex

READ:

How to Hedge Against a
Market Correction

TOPIC:
Common Hedging Techniques

URL and LINK:
See page 205

quite quickly through the use of stops, limit orders, short positions, inverse and leveraged positions, options and future. A good risk manager knows how (and when, very importantly) to use these instruments with confidence and prudence to avoid damaging losses.

Here's a checklist to use in your search for a good adviser:

- They place the focus on you and your goals, not how much money you're giving them.

- They patiently offer full and clear explanations to your questions, no matter how small or 'naïve'.

- They have thoughtful, intelligent responses if you bring up the themes discussed in *The Crash Course*. For example if you have concerns about the standard "buy and hold" meme, want to know if they take Peak Cheap Oil into account in their investment strategy, or want to consider allocating some of your portfolio into gold and silver, they don't dismiss or otherwise condescend to you (We find this is a pretty effective litmus test. PeakProsperity.com readers tend to find themselves quickly unhappy with advisers unwilling to discuss these themes seriously.)

- They're independently owned and operated. (Brokers at large firms are often pressured to place client funds into securities from which the parent firm makes more money.)

- They provide anytime access to your portfolio and its performance

- They have a track record of satisfactory returns over periods where the market is up, and excellent relative outperformance over periods where the market drops.

- They are in good regulatory standing and have no history of valid disclosures filed against them (complaints, arbitrations, regulatory actions, etc.). FINRA, the Financial Industry Regulatory Authority, offers a webtool that makes it simple to run a quick background check on any broker or firm at http://brokercheck.finra.org/

- Most important: they give you quality service and inspire your trust.

If you already have a trusted advisor in place, *Congratulations!* If not, time to get started finding one to partner with.

And if you find you have trouble locating one you feel comfortable with, we can help. We endorse a (very) short list of financial advisers with whom we have worked closely over the years and referred a number of Peak Prosperity readers to. We selected them for this very reason: many people were contacting us, hoping we could help connect them with professionals who look through a similar lens as we do. Apparently, there's a real dearth out there of advisers who share our concerns about the economy's blind assumption that economic growth will continue forever.

You can learn more about those advisers and request an initial, free consultation with them at www.greylockpeak.com.

Once you've recruited professional help on to your team, it's now time to get your perspective in the right place.

YOU MUST BE PREPARED TO LOSE MONEY

We're sorry to bear the news that Financial Repression is only one of a number of fronts on which your money is under siege.

Higher Taxes

As resource constraints increasingly restrict world economic growth, the interest demanded by our exponentially-expanding debts will start squeezing budgets ever-harder at both the Federal and municipal levels. And the response to this is incredibly easy to predict:

More taxes.

Like a drowning man, a fiscally-challenged government will grasp at anything—any revenue source it can lay it hands on—to avoid having to make itself smaller. And taxation is its easiest method of doing so.

Right now, income tax rates in the United States are near 80-year lows. The same is true of taxes on capital gains. So there's lots of room for scared politicians to raise both from here "in the national interest."

Expect to experience more taxation in the coming years, both through direct rate hikes as well as through "stealth" taxes like monetary inflation (which reduces the real cost to the government of making its debt interest and entitlement payments) or legislation like the Affordable Care Act (which has led to higher average health care premiums).

When it comes to stewarding your financial capital, working with a professional accountant (one with a CPA license) is strongly recommended. Employing legal ways to minimize your exposure to taxation is going to be a key pillar of building and retaining financial wealth over the next several decades. A good accountant will also work hand-in-hand with your financial adviser to develop and deploy a tax-advantaged investment strategy for you.

Lower Pensions

In addition to taxing more, as governments become more pinched for funds, they are also going to be forced to start spending less.

Right now, U.S. state public pensions are collectively underfunded by more than $1 trillion. And private sector pensions are underfunded by an even greater amount.

At the Federal level, the situation is even more dire than *that*. Estimates of the funding shortfall of entitlement programs like Social Security, Medicare and Medicaid range from—$60 trillion U.S. dollars to more than $200 hundred trillion.

These underfunded programs simply can't meet everything that's been promised. As budgets get tighter, funding for retirees and the unemployed will increasingly compete with infrastructure and commerce investment. When dollars are tight, will politicians spend what remains to create jobs, or pay people who aren't working? They will, predictably, go with the votes. This means that at first paying retirees will win out, but then later, the desire to create jobs will be stronger. That is, both groups will lose in the end by amounts equal to today's shortfalls which are, to be blunt, staggering.

The bottom line here is that if you are expecting to receive some sort of guaranteed payment from the government or employer when you retire, you'd better develop a contingency plan that assumes a good portion of it never arrives.

The Coming Bubble 'Pop!'

As we've mentioned, prices indicate that bubbles have re-emerged in the stock, bond and real estate markets, as well as many other investment classes from fine art to MLB season tickets. All courtesy of our friendly central bankers and their easy money.

And what do we know about bubbles? *They pop*. Remember what happened to investment portfolios and your house values between 2007-2009? It wasn't pretty.

None of the foundational culprits of the 2007/2008 crash have been effectively addressed and made safer. Indeed, nearly all have gotten worse. Compared to before the last crash: world debt is $57 trillion higher, world GDP growth is anemic, the "too big to fail" institutions that created the mess have only increased in size, and the crony relationship between our politicians and banking system has only become more entwined.

For the reasons we write about daily at PeakProsperity.com, many of which we've mentioned in this book, we are highly confident that a major crash—one that could cut prices in half or more—is in our near-term future (near-term defined as within the next five years). We realize that this may well be unpopular news. Many of us still feel like we've just picked ourselves off the floor after the knock-down blow the Great Recession dealt us, and we hate to be bearers of an unwelcome prediction like this. But we value realism, and sense you do, too, if you bought this book.

Which leads us to the title of this section: *Be Prepared To Lose Money.* Whether it's a market crash, a loss of income during the next recession, or just the slow erosion of wealth from financial repression and parasites like the high frequency trading computer robots that never fail to skim money from the markets for their owners, you have to get comfortable with the likely reality that events will conspire to make you lose money at times as we enter this turbulent future.

The trick to financial prosperity? *When those hard times arrive, make sure you lose **less** than everybody else.*

Our strongest advice is to then invest the money you've saved while prices are depressed and value can be bought on the cheap.

In order to be able to do this, it's critical for you to develop the emotional readiness now, in advance, to be able to buy "when there is blood in the streets" and not be paralyzed by the paper losses you will be sure to have taken when that moment arrives. Accepting these losses now, before they have happened, will prevent you from being overwhelmed or panicking when they actually occur, as well as give you the clarity of purpose to act when most others are too stunned or too fearful to do so.

Yes, it sounds strange. But for this reason, we firmly believe that making peace with losing money is an essential step towards ultimately accumulating a lot more of it.

FIRST DEFLATION, THEN INFLATION

This emotional readiness is going to serve you well as the approaching set of crises discussed in Chapter 2 fully get underway. Things are going to get very rocky, and very confusing. Most people will simply hunker down during this time, and not realize what's happened to them and their wealth until the transfer is completed.

So understanding the likely course of coming events is hugely important, and can give you a tremendous advantage. Because you'll know what signs to look for and what to do when you see them.

The Ka-POOM! Theory

What the 2008 financial crisis made clear is that when natural market forces want to purge the oversupply of poor-quality debt from the system they do exactly that. The bad mortgages (think subprime), the bad sovereign debts (think Greece), and the loan portfolios of over-extended financial institutions (think Citibank) represented "poor quality debt." When the market (finally) figured out that those debts would never be repaid at face value, or perhaps at all, turmoil erupted.

During times like these, the market demands higher interest rates for the increased risks it sees. But this makes debts harder to service, ultimately triggering defaults, which only compounds the difficulties of the issuers of low quality debt, as interest costs and defaults spiral ever upwards until the system is purged. Think of it as nature's way of removing bad credit from the world, the way a lion chases the lamest antelope first.

Because in our fiat currency system "all money is loaned into existence" (see chapters 7 and 8 of *The Crash Course* on-line video series), during periods of high debt default, the money supply shrinks. This is the textbook definition of deflation—a common symptom of which is falling prices—meaning there is less money (and/or credit) available to chase goods and services.

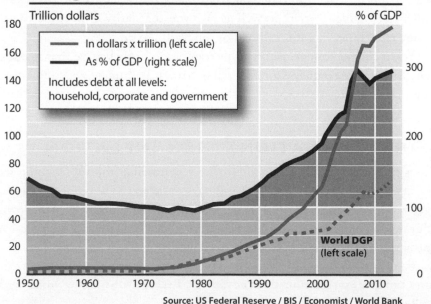

Total global credit-market debt owed

Source: US Federal Reserve / BIS / Economist / World Bank

This is what we saw of course, as the last financial crisis struck in 2008: Prices fell hard across stocks, bonds, real estate, and a wide number of other asset classes.

The "recovery" we've experienced since then is primarily due to the world's central banks acting in unison, printing over $10 trillion to buy up huge tranches of this lame, limping debt and holding it so that it can't be declared in default—essentially preventing nature from having its due (for the time being).

This thwarting of the natural order can't last forever for a number of reasons, a big one being that the system went right back to its reckless ways, unsurprisingly, after the central banks rode to its rescue. In the years since the excessive highs of 2008, global credit-market debt has increased by another $57 trillion, on track to soon top $200 trillion in total.

The year 2008 was a wake-up call to change our ways, but as a society we didn't listen at all. Instead, we've responded by doing more of the same behavior that created the crisis in the first place. That's a sure-fire recipe for repeating the same downfall, just from a higher elevation next time.

This is a main reason why we have great confidence that deflation will once again gain the upper hand in the future. Nature can only be denied for so long.

This is why we subscribe to the *Ka-POOM!* theory, originally coined by economist Eric Janszen in 1998 (who later re-named it The Janszen Scenario). Its name is inspired by the dual nature of most explosions: first a detonation creates a shock wave (the *Ka!*) inside the financial matrix which first compresses it initiating a chain reaction, and then quickly morphs into a massive pressure build-up that explodes in a shock wave that spreads outwards in all directions at hypersonic speeds (the *POOM!*).

Janzen's theory forecasts that our twin burden of too much debt combined with overinflated asset prices will reach a tipping point, where buyers of both debt and equity go on strike. A deflationary crunch (the *Ka!*) is the first of this two-act play, creating a vicious cycle of defaults, corporate layoffs and portfolio losses, which only make buyers retrench even further. The mal-investments are hunted down and eaten by financial predators.

This period will be experienced by most as a brutal time, and will look and feel similar to the last financial crisis, only worse. It's important to remember that within just five short months after the crisis hit in October 2008, the Dow Jones index had dropped by over 50% and the labor market had shed over 4 million jobs. Again, given that conditions today are even more overextended on many fronts, the carnage wreaked by this coming deflation will likely be worse.

Of course this will send our central leaders and policymakers into panic. Shouts of *"Do something, anything!"* will come from politicians and voters alike. All eyes will look to the central bankers to *"Do whatever it takes"* to make the collapse stop. And they will respond using the only weapon they have: the printing press.

Concluding that their previous quantitative easing (QE) programs were effective but simply not large enough, they will turn the presses on overdrive in order to prop up prices and end the defaults. Former Federal Reserve Chairman Ben Bernanke once quasi-joked of dropping money from helicopters to combat deflation—the *Ka-POOM!* scenario is the sort of one he was referring to. The Fed would become the buyer of last resort, purchasing huge percentages of the bond market, the stock market, and home mortgages. In addition to supporting the banks, it would probably send stimulus directly to citizens, either as checks or in the form of future income tax forgiveness and/or prior year rebates. That is, they would try and print their way out of trouble.

This explosion of new "thin-air" money (the *POOM!* part of the cycle) will be highly inflationary and if large enough will temporarily stop and reverse the fall in asset prices. But in so doing, the purchasing power of the currency will be viciously and rapidly diminished. So we expect the central banks to "win the battle" for a while, but ultimately lose the war.

Savers will be destroyed. Prices will skyrocket—this will actually not be the result of things becoming more expensive, but of people's faith in money eroding. Fear of holding currency will grow, as citizens rightly worry that its rapid depreciation will continue. The velocity of money will skyrocket and just as happened in Weimer Germany in the 1920s, Yugoslavia in the early 1990s, Zimbabwe in the 2000s, and as is happening now in countries like Argentina and Venezuela, the populace will lose confidence in the value of its currency. Once that happens hyperinflation results, exposing the fact that the majority of paper money's value comes from confidence and nothing more.

In hyperinflation, a currency becomes essentially worthless; so much of it has been printed that no one wants it, and therefore it fails to be either a means of exchange or a store of value—the two basic functions money must perform.

TRANSITION INTO TANGIBLE ASSETS

This likely progression into currency collapse is critical to understand, as several key conclusions can be drawn from it. The most important being: move your financial assets from paper investments into real things before the trouble begins!

Tangible assets, often referred to as "hard assets," are things like land, commodities, finished goods, and productive enterprises. These things cannot be magically increased at will, as can currency with a printing press and so they preserve actual wealth. This has always proven to be true throughout history.

As prices become more and more distorted by central bank policies, the true value of tangible assets remains constant. A stand of timber has an intrinsic value, no matter how much or how little the *price* of lumber is. It is because of this feature that tangible assets serve as a good store of value in the way that money should (but routinely does not).

> **LISTEN:**
>
> 🎙️
>
> **Philip Haslam Podcast**
>
> **TOPIC:** Hyperinflation in Zimbabwe
>
> **URL and LINK:** See page 205

This means that in times when our currency is failing us (but really it's our leadership failing us), the desire to hold tangible assets grows. Those holding hard assets not only protect their purchasing power, but are often offered attractive premiums by potential buyers at key moments who are increasingly desperate to own some hard assets of their own.

Move to Own Primary and Secondary Assets

We expect that there's going to be a massive shift in the concentration of financial wealth back into more tangible forms of wealth.

We'll talk in more detail about this in the chapter on Living Capital, but we agree with E.F. Schumacher who viewed financial wealth as being divided into three principal forms: primary, secondary and tertiary.

Primary wealth consists of raw natural resources: timber, farmland, fisheries, mineral ores, etc.

Secondary wealth is comprised of the goods and services that result through the transformation of primary wealth: lumber, food, steel, productive businesses, etc.

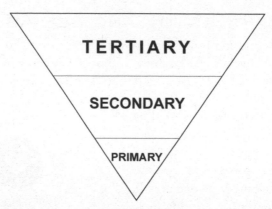

Tertiary assets like stocks and bonds, however, are simply paper *claims* on secondary and primary forms of wealth. Without those more fundamentals assets, tertiary wealth would have no meaning, no value, and would not exist. And if we look at the number of those tertiary paper claims, and the ways in which these claims have been greatly multiplied through the use of leverage and derivatives (American banks alone have over $280 trillion in derivatives on their books) we quickly compute that the vast majority of tertiary assets are unsecured "phantom wealth." *There are simply way more claims on "real stuff" than there is "real stuff."*

So in essence, tertiary wealth is only worth what people are willing to accept for the paper currency it's denominated in. But, at the end of the day, what people actually want is to be able to exchange their claims for 'stuff.' What will happen when people's preferences shift from wanting to hold paper claims to wanting to hold real things? The perceived worth of tertiary assets will evaporate. No one will want to hold stock or bonds or derivatives or even currency itself if things get bad enough.

This is why we predict the eventual shift of financial capital from paper into things.

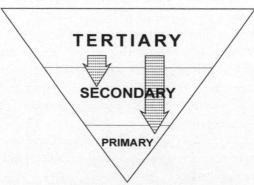

In fact, it's already happening if you know where to look. The top 1% are quite busy exchanging their tertiary wealth for land, for fine art, for trophy properties and other assets that are finite, desirable and discrete. For example, at the end of 2014, it was revealed that Microsoft billionaire Bill Gates has quietly amassed one of the largest portfolios of farmland in the U.S. Southeast. And it's not just rich individuals; a number of hedge funds and indeed nations, via their sovereign wealth funds, are following suit.

So, how does the average individual start moving a portion of their financial wealth out of tertiary capital and into tangible assets?

Sell Claims and Build Cash

The first step is easy. Sell some of your stock and bond positions. Determine a starting percentage—5%, 10%—and hit the sell button (deciding how much to liquidate and which positions to sell is, of course, best determined with the guidance of your professional adviser).

It is worth talking for a moment about the wisdom of holding cash in this environment, despite our near-term concerns about financial repression and our long-term ones that the currency is likely to get debased.

First, we have yet to enter the *Ka-POOM!* phase. All of that likely madness is still ahead of us. In the here and now, as discussed, we are increasingly seeing bubble pricing in markets. And what happens with bubbles? They pop. When they do, prices drop and cash then buys a lot more than it did before the bursting. Unless you have a gambler's mindset with your savings, having a substantial portion of your financial portfolio in cash right now seems quite prudent to us.

Second, once we do enter the *Ka!* Phase—which may come with the popping of these latest bubbles, or not (no one can predict with certainty)—the deflationary price downdraft will be vicious. All asset prices, tangible assets, too, will suffer. This is the "blood in the streets" moment you've heard about. At this time, cash will be of paramount importance. Both as a store of value, and as 'dry powder' to deploy in purchasing excellent primary and secondary assets on the cheap.

So, specifically, we recommend the following with cash:

- **Step1: Build an emergency stash** – this should be in physical bills, kept outside of the banking system (home safe, etc). This is money for a true emergency, like a surprise shut-down of the electrical grid or banking system. It's for you to trade for supplies or pay transport costs if you need to get to a safer location. Our recommendation is to ultimately have $2,000 per family member.

- **Step 2: Keep a reserve for hard times** – this is your savings to help cushion against a surprise loss of income (job loss, etc.). We recommend working to save up three to six months worth of your current income in cash, out of the banking system.

- **Step 3: Build your dry powder** – this is the capital you will use for purchasing tangible assets at attractive prices. Which assets and at what prices is, again, best arrived at in partnership with a good adviser. We recommend taking a measured approach here. Don't rush to deploy this cash unless certain conditions (which we'll mention soon) occur.

- **Step 4: Diversify your other holdings** – No one knows for certain what the future will bring. Holding a core position (say 10% of your financial wealth) in cash gives you a safety margin, some portfolio diversification, and preserves some options for you if the future ends up surprising us all. Your diversified positions can be, and if large enough *should* be, diversified into multiple currencies and cash equivalents (e.g., Treasury bills) for further safety.

There are a few notable risks with cash to be aware of.

One is the risk of a **bank bail-in** when the next financial crisis arrives. A "bail-in" occurs when the government determines a failing bank can only meet its obligations to various creditors by deploying depositors' funds. In a bail-in, your savings are essentially used to pay for the banks misdeeds and bad decisions. This type of bank rescue occurred in Cyprus in 2013, and many think this was a test-run for future such situations elsewhere in the West. Indeed, the G20 decided in November 2014 that any deposits above the federally-insured limit will be subordinate to most creditor claims of a failing bank including, remarkably, any losing derivative bets your bank may have made

Yes, even though it's *your* money, the rules have been changed to give others senior rights to it during times of trouble. Not so coincidentally, every single one of the recent rule changes have been made *against* you and *for* the banks and their betting partners.

So, if your cash balances are large enough, we recommend you spread them out across several banks, always keeping the balance in each account under the federally insured level ($250,000 per individual account in the United States, but $100,000 would be safer as that's the old limit).

Fortunately, the trouble that hit the banking system in Cyprus and other hard-hit nations, like Greece, did not happen overnight. We believe we'll be able to observe warning signs in advance, and if we do, we will issue an alert through PeakProsperity.com if we become concerned enough about the stability of the major United States and European banking systems that considering taking your actual cash notes out of the bank is warranted.

The other big risk with cash will arrive with the *POOM!* phase discussed earlier. Once the deflationary tide has been reversed, the ensuing hyperinflationary flood will destroy cash's purchasing power. This is another scenario in which we will issue a PeakProsperity.com alert to *run*, not walk, to exchange all of your cash for tangible assets. Again, it's highly unlikely this will be an overnight development; and we'll have the proceeding *Ka!* phase as our wake-up call. But it's an eventuality we all must remain vigilant for.

Own Precious Metals

With such dire talk of inflation, deflation and currency crisis, it should come as little surprise that we are big advocates of owning precious metals.

Our rationale why could fill an entire book in itself. Indeed, we've written extensively on the topic at PeakProsperity.com for many years. But simply put, we are keen on owning precious metals—gold and silver, primarily—for two principle reasons.

The first is they are among the easiest tangible assets to own. Buying real estate, a business, or collectibles like fine art requires a substantial investment of time and due diligence; whereas gold and silver bullion can be purchased within minutes from a reliable vendor. They require no management, are easy and inexpensive to store, and do not spoil. They are the "gateway drug" into tangible asset investing.

The second is that gold and silver have served successfully and effectively as money since the dawn of human history. This thousands-year-old streak is not likely to end anytime soon, despite our historically recent experiment with un-backed (also known as "fiat") paper currency.

As hard assets, precious metals promise to hold their value well during times of economic turmoil (in fact, during these times they often enjoy a 'safety' premium). On top of this, they also have potential to be one day re-monetized: to be used as backing for one or more major world currencies. Should one or more of the major fiat currencies fail, it would not be unlikely at all for a return to some form of gold standard to be called for. It's pretty much the only historically-stable alternative the world knows of. Were this to happen, the perceived value of gold would likely rise much, much higher from where it is today given the relatively small volume of gold above the ground compared to today's world money supplies.

For these principle reasons, we recommend that everyone strongly consider:

- **Establishing a foundational position in gold and silver**. This is your Armageddon insurance against a currency crisis and general meltdown of the financial system. If you're new to precious metals investing, this should be a minimum of 5% of your financial portfolio, though 10% or more is reasonable given where we are in this particular story of monetary madness.

- **Buying physical bullion**, not "paper gold" like ETFs or mining stocks. Take delivery of the metal yourself or have it stored somewhere you have confidence is secure. If stored remotely, make sure the metal is owned outright in your name (referred to as "allocated" storage), as opposed to having a claim on bullion that is pooled together ("unallocated" storage).

- **Increasing your exposure over time**. There are many ways above owning physical bullion to invest in precious metals. For those with their foundational position already in place, expanding into these other forms of ownership offers access to greater wealth creation when capital starts fleeing the tertiary levels of wealth looking for safety. As an unadulterated form of primary wealth with universal acceptability, durability, portability and divisibility, the precious metals are the ultimate crisis safe haven for financial capital.

As mentioned, precious metals are a large focus area of our work at PeakProsperity.com. We've created several helpful resources there for you to learn more:

- Guide on which forms of precious metals to buy
  http://www.peakprosperity.com/buying_gold

- Reputable places to buy precious metals
  http://www.peakprosperity.com/where-to-buy-gold-and-silver

- Gold & Silver discussion group
  http://www.peakprosperity.com/group/gold-silver

Invest in Sustainable Ventures

With the financial capital you have remaining, we strongly consider investing it in businesses that own, produce and manage primary or secondary forms of wealth. Again, here's where a good financial adviser who understands the Three Es will play an invaluable role in providing guidance.

Sectors we think worthy of consideration include:

- Real estate (especially farmland and timberland)

- Oil and gas exploration and production
- Resource mining companies
- Water infrastructure and utilities
- Smart grid/electrical power transmission
- Small to mid-size local businesses providing essential services

Your financial adviser should be able to find plenty of publicly-traded candidates in these sectors with strong balance sheets for you consider.

In addition, for accredited investors (as defined by the SEC), there are an increasing number of opportunities emerging for investing privately in these sectors. A few that have caught our attention over the years are:

- **Farmland LP**: a fund that upgrades conventionally-farmed fields to organic status, managing them thereafter using sustainable practices

- **Slow Money**: invests private capital in local food systems across the United States

- **CircleUp.com**: invests private capital in early-stage innovative consumer product and retail companies

LISTEN: Woody Tasch Podcast TOPIC: The Slow Money Movement URL and LINK: See page 205	LISTEN: Farmland LP Podcast TOPIC: Investing in Farmland, Sustainably URL and LINK: See page 206

Invest Locally

For many reading this, some of your best options for moving capital into secondary or primary forms of wealth will be within a 10-mile radius of where you live.

Buying into local businesses or property holds much potential for those looking to diversify out of traditional stocks and bonds. First off, it keeps your money out of the Wall Street casino, offering you greater visibility and control as to how your investment capital is put to work. Imagine: if enough of us eventually do this, our collective starvation of that beast might just sufficiently de-fang it and free our society from its jaws.

In addition to attractive profits, investing in local businesses yields additional returns Wall Street cannot offer. Keeping your capital local allows entrepreneurs in your area to create value, value that benefits your community, increasing its overall state of resilience. A regression analysis published in the *Harvard Business Review* (2010) calculated that communities with the highest local businesses per capita enjoyed the highest probability of per capita job growth.

Even the Federal Reserve agrees. In September 2013, the Atlanta Fed released a study of all U.S. counties, concluding that those with the highest concentration of local businesses had the highest per capita income and the highest probability of eradicating poverty. When the next economic downturn hits, the presence and use of local capital is going to be a principal determinant of how your city fares.

Investing your capital locally also increases your perceived value within your community. Your visibility as a supporter of the local economy is appreciated by entrepreneurs and customers alike. It's a distinction that increases your social value: when tough times hit, you've demonstrated that you're the kind of person the community is better off with than without.

So, lots of good reasons exist to direct a portion of your Financial Future Portfolio into investments in your local area. But how, exactly to do it?

Being honest, it's substantially harder today to invest locally than it is on Wall Street. That's just the reality of where we are in this story. You can buy a publicly traded stock or bond with the click of a mouse. Identifying local investments, doing your due diligence, and arranging terms with your potential new partners, however, takes time and effort. Often a lot of it. And while there are start-ups working hard to create exchanges to bring local capital together with local businesses, the experience will likely never be as immediate and effortless as buying a stock on the NYSE.

But perhaps that's a good thing. We've all been sold on the narrative that investing is easy: All you do is press the buy button, then hold for the long run (and along the way: Buy the dips!) and everything will turn out just fine. Well, in reality, investing is much more complicated than that, or otherwise everyone would already be rich.

Given the more turbulent future we predict is ahead of us, perhaps *all* investments should be preceded with a fundamental examination of the strategy, plan and talent behind them. The local investing model may just have a lot to teach the financial community.

If you don't have relationships with many local businesses, your city's Chamber of Commerce is a good place to start for a directory of those in your area. These Chambers often arrange regular meetings of their members, which you can either attend or ask if your name would be circulated as someone interested in contributing capital to a local venture. Bank loan officers are also good contacts to make, as they have good visibility into which nearby companies are raising funds.

Here are several good books containing *How To?* specifics on investing locally:

- *Local Dollars, Local Sense: How To Shift Your Money From Wall Street To Main Street and Achieve Real Prosperity*, Michael Shuman (2012)
- *Locavesting: The Revolution In Local Investing And How To Profit From It* Amy Cortese (2011)

Resilience Investing

And don't forget about your Resilience Fund! That's the money you've left aside to exchange for other forms of capital that will increase your overall resilience.

In addition to enhancing your ability to weather future surprises, many of these other types of capital yield excellent financial returns. For example, energy production or efficiency systems often yield tremendous cost savings over their lifetimes. A solar hot water heater can often have a financial ROI well over 100%. Similarly, investing in your health, wellness and fitness (such as a nutritionist consultation, therapist, CrossFit membership, etc) can save you thousands of dollars and perhaps add years to your lifespan.

We'll have more specifics about how to best deploy your Resilience Funds over the other 8 Forms in the chapters that follow.

PRIORITIZE CASH FLOW

We're big fans of investing your capital, locally or otherwise, in opportunities that produce positive cash flows.

We've spent time with a number of successful investors and entrepreneurs, and this preference for cash flow is a common trait they all clearly share. Investment author Robert Kiyosaki believes so strongly that good cash flows are the key to financial wealth that he gambled everything at the start of his career on a game, *CASHFLOW*, he and his wife Kim created to teach people about them. His best-selling book *Rich Dad Poor Dad* is basically a beefed-up version of the game's instruction manual (one that has sold over 35 million copies!).

Invest in Assets with Positive Cash Flows

As you deploy your capital, locally or otherwise, we encourage you to place a higher preference on opportunities that generate positive cash flows versus those that merely "promise" future price appreciation.

During the deflationary phase predicted by the *Ka-POOM!* theory, prices of nearly all assets should be pushed downwards. That will be much less of a problem if the asset is producing a positive cash flow. While, yes, the price of your investment may have lost money on paper, that only matters if you sell it. If instead you can hold onto it and use the cash flow you receive to weather this lean time, when the inflationary *POOM!* phase hits later on, you'll likely have the chance to sell the asset (only if you want to, of course) at a higher price down the road.

But if the asset doesn't produce cash for you, like most of today's high P/E tech stock darlings, things can be much more dire.

First, during a deflationary rout, all prices fall. But the prices of unprofitable assets fall most. Nobody wants to hold a money pit when money is scarce.

And second, you may be forced to sell the asset during this rocky time. Maybe you fear the asset is on its way to becoming worthless, and you want to get at least some of your capital back. Or you lose your job, have unexpected expenses to pay or, God-forbid, have margin calls to meet. Without positive cash flows to sustain you during this period, you have few options but selling if you need the money. And when you liquidate the asset, you lock in the loss. At that point, the money you've lost is gone for good.

Develop Multiple Streams of Income

Most people have all of their eggs in one basket when it comes to income. If the family bread-winner loses their job, most if not all income to the household stops.

Sadly, expenses do not. And without income, expenses start chewing through savings very quickly.

Remember the personal Income Statement and Balance Sheet we created at the beginning of this chapter? Given yours, how long could you sustain your household if your main source of income suddenly disappeared? Three months? Six months? More? Less?

Your best defense against sudden income loss—due to recession, layoff, firing, injury, whatever—is having multiple income streams in place. Earlier we talked about *redundancy* as an important component of resilience, such like that seen in animals that give birth to large litters. This is the same concept.

With multiple income streams, if you lose one, you still have the others to sustain you.

And even if the source of the majority of your income disappears, having 20-30% of your prior income level is vastly better than having 0% of it. Having *some* income allows you to pare your expenses down to the bare essentials and perhaps still be solvent and self-supporting. Having *none* precludes those options.

So how does one create an additional stream of income? There's no one-size-fits-all answer to this question. It depends on your skills, interests, strengths, resources and appetite for risk.

But there are methodologies you can follow to identify opportunities that will be a good fit. Working with a mentor or a professional adviser, like a qualified career or life coach, who can walk you through the structured exploration, is recommended. As is reading a few of the many, many books available on the topic, if for no other reason than getting additional exposure to potential income-generating ideas to consider.

New income streams can be any size and require anywhere from 0 to 20+ hours per week. You can earn them with your labor and expertise (such as starting a weekend lawn care service), or purchase them with your investment capital (like buying a rental property). Again, your personal circumstances will determine what's best for you to pursue.

But our advice is to leverage your strengths and diversify. If you've developed mastery of a skill (Sales, for example) that one employer is already paying you for, then others are likely to pay you for it, too. If all of your income streams have the same risk exposure, the likelihood they could all get compromised at the same time increases.

This isn't empty guidance. Both Chris and Adam have worked to create income streams of varying sizes across different lines of business to supplement their base earnings from running Peak Prosperity. While their 'day job' provides each with their largest income stream, should it go away for some (hopefully incredibly low probability) reason, these other cash flows should keep them afloat while they determine what to do next.

Your next supplemental income source should fit in the overlap of what you *want to* do, what you *can* do, what you have *time* to do, and what you can *afford* to do. Once you've identified the opportunity, pilot the idea with a few potential employers/customers and then iterate from there based on the feedback you receive.

Amass Passive Income

Active income is earned based on the sweat of your brow. Most salaried jobs fit in this category. If you don't go into work, you don't get paid.

Passive income is earned by your financial capital. Essentially, this is your money working for you, while you sleep in or attend to other things in life.

The financially wealthy primarily make their cash flow from passive income, from the earnings produced by their investment portfolios. Indeed, a common measure of becoming "rich" or "financially free" is reaching the milestone where your annual passive income exceeds your annual living expenses. At this point, you're free to spend your time however you like, without the worry of unpaid bills.

This is a good goal to strive for with your financial capital. Even if you never attain "financial freedom," having more and more of your expenses offset by passive investments with positive cash flows will make your financial life easier and easier over time. The difference in effort and stress between having to actively work to fund 100% of your expenses versus 25% of them is very large.

The most common sources of passive cash flows are from investments in blue-chip stocks (dividends), bonds (coupon payments), business ownership, rental real estate properties, franchises, and royalties/licensing (from books, music, product patents, etc.).

A good financial adviser can help guide you in how to find and evaluate opportunities in many of these categories to determine if they may be right for you. Successful investing in this space takes capital and expertise. Pursue opportunities over time with a "slow and steady" approach and an eye to risk-minimization. Smaller, safer investments will accrete over time to create a sizable passive income stream—without the risk involved in big "swing for the fences" bets.

MANAGE DEBT VERY CAREFULLY

Be very, very careful with debt in the coming years.

During deflation, the real cost of debt increases. If you lose your income during this time and can't service your interest payments, debt then becomes a stone-cold killer.

In general, we recommend living a debt-free lifestyle whenever possible.

We can say with certainty that "unproductive" debt should be avoided whenever possible. This is debt that doesn't increase your odds of earning more income in the future. It's usually consumptive in nature, like charging your vacation expenses on your credit card. We pretty much don't like any kind of credit card or auto loans, and we generally advise people to pay down their mortgages whenever able to.

Increasingly, we also see most student debt as detrimental. Tuition costs have far outpaced the value that today's university degrees are worth, creating a generation of debt serfs. Unless you have high confidence you know you will be earning enough out of school to afford the cost of the degree, taking out large student loans is a bad idea. There are an increasing number of innovative ways to educate yourself at affordable cost, albeit unconventionally.

We're less allergic to "productive" debt, as long as it has a high probability of enabling you ultimately to earn more than you borrowed. An example of productive debt is a mortgage taken out to purchase real estate you plan to lease. If you can lease it out for more than your monthly mortgage payment, thereby letting the renter pay your mortgage off for you over time, that's worth seriously considering. Just run the numbers to calculate that if prices crash and you're forced to sell at a loss, it won't be one large enough to ruin you.

People ask us frequently that if high inflation wins out eventually, won't debt burdens be inflated away? The short answer is "yes," but a very cautious one. We're not advising folks to leverage themselves to the hilt, counting on high inflation to save them. As we emphasize, no one knows the exact path things will take, and you don't want to be caught with a lot of debt at the wrong time. That way lies ruin.

Though, there may come a time, at the turn from the *Ka!* phase into the *POOM!,* when it will make sense to take out low-cost debt and buy productive, tangible assets with it. The burst of inflation should make the cost of servicing your debt much lower as time goes on, while the prices of your assets rise.

We will be keeping our eyes out closely for that, and if/when the time does occur, we'll issue an alert to our subscribers on PeakProsperity.com.

LIVE BELOW YOUR MEANS AND INVEST THE DIFFERENCE

At the end of the day, the less we want, the less we need. As Ralph Waldo Emerson eloquently praised Henry David Thoreau back in 1862:

"He chose to be rich by making his wants few, and supplying them himself."

We should all aspire to such an approach to wealth. Happiness is not how many dollars you have to your name. Rather it's about your ability to satisfy your wants dependably.

As we close this long chapter (don't worry, the rest are a lot shorter), we should remember that Financial Capital is only money.

And Money ≠ Resilience.

Instead, resilience results from wealth across all 8 Forms of Capital. With Financial Capital now taken care of, let's start developing the remaining seven.

CHAPTER 7

LIVING CAPITAL

In many people's lives, a connection to the natural world has almost disappeared. Daily contact with the outdoor world has been reduced to a scant few seconds between the car door and our front door. Because of this limited exposure, it's easy to forget that humans remain 100% dependent on natural systems for our survival.

This is a fact we only fleetingly remember when nature misbehaves, like when it forgets to drop rain on California or forces Australia to invent new "maximum hot" colors for its national heat index map or breaks eastern US snowfall records with impunity.

Those paying closer attention, however, are very worried by the clear and multiplying signs indicating that the stable natural systems we rely upon are faltering. Nature has limits and we are rubbing up against them. If we push past those limits, science tells us our ecosystems will quickly shift from their current states of complexity to different and probably less useful ones. That process usually isn't beneficial for humans. Rainforests could become deserts, fertile prairie topsoils might become sterile hardpan, and ocean fisheries could turn into jellyfish factories.

For our own sakes, and for the sake of future generations, we need to change our relationship with nature from one that is destructive to one that is *regenerative.*

We need nature's beauty and bounty every bit as much today as we did thousands of years ago. It feeds us, clothes us, shelters us, and its building blocks quite literally make us who are. Biologically, we are hard-wired to be outside. Study after study have shown the physical and mental benefits of regular, outdoor activity for children and adults alike.

Improving and regenerating the Living Capital in your life is an exceptionally important part of your resilience plan and attending to it will provide surprising improvements in your health and enjoyment of life.

So what is Living Capital? It's the water in our streams, lakes, ponds and aquifers. It's healthy soils teeming with microbes. It's insects, birds, mammals and it is our own human bodies.

Any of us can work to increase and improve the living capital around and within us. The good news is that this is not only completely within our power, but it's also rewarding and satisfying. We can all be regenerative if we put our minds to it. And the benefits we receive—better health, more dependable food supplies, more beauty around us, and more productive lands—enrich us in ways that lead to a more enjoyable and possibly longer life.

LET'S MAKE A DEAL

Living Capital is mainly built up by careful effort, but you can also swap Financial Capital for Living Capital. Both Chris and Adam regularly exchange money for compost, fruit trees, bee packages, soil, berry bushes, plants, gardens and seeds. They also use money to eat well (which isn't always cheap if you are buying organic or locally fresh foods), to belong to fitness gyms, and to obtain high-quality medical data used fine-tune their individual health needs.

Trading money or time for Living Capital is both easy and immensely satisfying. With a relatively minor investment of cash and/or effort you can rapidly improve the soils around your property, increase the number of pollinators by planting their preferred food sources, become more fit, and produce an abundance of food that will feed humans and animals alike.

If you do this, in a surprisingly short amount of time, you can find yourself as we do: healthier and surrounded by productive abundance and beauty. In our lives, that means gardens that bloom across multiple seasons, flocks and herds of farm stock, well-pruned trees that bear fruit and flowers, rich soils, and living in proximity to a diversity of wildlife.

Depending on where you live, it may be an entirely different combination of natural bounty, but whatever your situation, the opportunity to re-connect with nature in a way that serves you and enriches the biosphere is there for the taking.

ANOTHER (WRONG) CULTURAL NARRATIVE

As we've discussed earlier, having the right story in place is essential to making good decisions. If you have the wrong narrative running you'll get bad results.

One of the most unfortunate (and wrong) elements of our modern narrative is probably this one: *Humans destroy nature.* It's not so much a judgment as it is a belief. Nature provides and people consume. Or so the story goes.

We've been conditioned to believe that when humans move in nature will suffer; species will be depleted if not entirely made extinct. Waters will be stripped of fish and fouled. Soils will be depleted, if not entirely lost. Forests will be leveled; and natural areas will shrink and shrink and shrink until they're all but gone.

As our friend James Howard Kunstler likes to put it, when you see the bulldozers arrive at the field across the street, you just know something ugly is about to happen.

In this view, it's as if humans are a blight upon the land; consumers destined to eat up everything and leave wastelands in their path. Give us enough time and we'll just ruin the natural world, locally first, and then possibly globally, as the climate change data suggests.

But it doesn't *have* to go that way. Your authors believed the standard narrative for most of their lives, too—that is, until we saw people proving the opposite. Things can go in an entirely different and dazzling direction.

Humans can be agents of incredible regeneration and abundance. We can speed up the creation of topsoil by a factor of more than 100x over what nature can do alone. We can create a healthy mature forest in a fraction of the time versus the natural growth rate.

We can be agents of incredibly positive change and abundance *especially* when it comes to Living Capital. That is, the story that humans are destroyers of nature is not just wrong, it also leaves out the reality that we can be stewards and the creators of extraordinary abundance.

Your considerable intellect can do amazing things when directed at the world around you, including the natural world. While, yes, the default seems to have been careless destruction for a very long time, it's important to note that this default operating position is not the same thing as *destiny*. We not only can do better, we *should* do better.

SINGING FROGS FARM

The farming model being pioneered at Singing Frogs Farm, a small micro-farm in northern California, is one such example of doing things "right." By combining bio-intensive land and forestry management theory with empirical trial and error, the farming practices at Singing Frogs have produced astounding results.

First off and most importantly, no tilling of any kind is done to the soil. No pesticide/herbicide/fungicide sprays (organic or otherwise) are used, and the only fertilizer used is natural compost.

These practices have resulted in a build-up of nutrient-dense, highly bio-rich topsoil. Where most farms have less than 12 inches of "alive" topsoil in which they can grow things, Singing Frogs' extends to a depth over four feet(!).

This high-carbon layer of soil retains much more water than conventional topsoil, requiring much less irrigation than used at most farms, a very important factor given the historic drought the West is currently suffering.

All these advantages combine to enable Singing Frogs Farm to produce five to seven harvests per year on their land, vs. the one to two harvest average of other farms. And since the annual crop yield is so much higher, so is the revenue. Most other farms in northern California average $14,000 in gross revenue per acre. Singing Frogs grosses nearly $100,000 per acre—a stunning *seven times* more.

If we can do things the right way like the folks at Singing Frogs Farm, earn more money, and make the world a healthier place, the only question is why *aren't* we?

The way permaculture experts Ethan Roland and Gregory Landua put it in their book *Regenerative Enterprise*, we need to shift away from thinking of nature as some vast *extractive* enterprise and towards thinking *regeneratively*.

The beauty of it all is, both our bodies and the natural world are primed and ready for this. All we have to do is work with them as they are. That is, we need to be in relationship *with* our Living Capital, not trying to force our will upon it.

LISTEN:

Singing Frogs Farm
Podcast

TOPIC:
Soil Management

URL and LINK:
See page 206

IT STARTS WITH A HEALTHY BODY

Advising people to get healthy is a no-brainer recommendation; one that we're going to make as well.

What we want to add to the conversation is the idea that being in shape will be an essential element to successfully thriving in some future scenarios. We note that being out of shape reveals the underlying assumptions that the future will be relatively easy and benign, with the same comfortable lifestyles and easy access to medical care when and if needed. In our view, those are flawed assumptions.

Instead, we should consider the current period of ease and stability to be a transient artifact of the age of petroleum, something that we know will be drawing to a close at some point. Given that, doesn't it make sense to begin acting as if it's already true, and that the right time to get in peak physical condition is now?

When this light bulb sparked on in the brains of your authors, they both applied basic science and good old-fashioned discipline to dramatically improve their general levels of health and fitness. Following prudent exercise and nutrition regimes, Chris shed 40 pounds, and Adam 30. As of this writing, we're both in the best all-round physical condition of our lives.

By our own personal trans-formations, we've learned first-hand that better health is not only a great strategy for meeting the future, but it enables us to do more and enjoy life more *today*. We're more capable, energetic and happier than we were before. And we have a greater confidence that as long as we maintain our good health, we'll fare better in the face of whatever the future brings our way.

READ:

The New Me

TOPIC:
Chris' Personal Health Transformation

URL and LINK:
See page 206

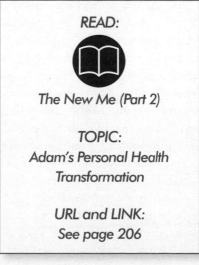

READ:

The New Me (Part 2)

TOPIC:
Adam's Personal Health Transformation

URL and LINK:
See page 206

If you feel you could benefit from a similar path as we've taken, the most important elements to focus on are:

- **Nutrition** – Everything rests on good nutrition. Not only does this deliver the essential nutrients your body needs to function properly, but it's also the key to weight loss. In addition, it's your most effective vehicle for reducing the inflammation and toxins responsible for aging, injury and disease. Eat poorly and it does not matter how much exercise you do, you will still be unhealthy.

- **Physical activity** – Focus on developing strength, flexibility, endurance and co-ordination. We recommend fitness programs like CrossFit that promote high-intensity, multi-varied exercises for supervised coaching and effective results. The key is regular, daily, exercise, even if that means just 10 minutes of sit ups and push ups between rounds at your computer.

- **Sleep** – The benefits of sufficient sleep are many, and the cost of too little can range from chronic fatigue and lack of focus, to weight gain, to greater risk of diabetes and heart attack. Sadly, over 75% of Americans experience some form of chronic sleep disorder.

- **Stress reduction** – Stress is a killer and our modern lifestyle is full of it. It weakens our immune systems, ages us, affects our weight, teeth, and temperament. Finding ways to minimize stress' ability to take root in our bodies and minds—with mindfulness, meditation, yoga, etc.—is well worth the time invested.

All of the above are important in your pursuit of better health. And improving one of them will usually help with improving the others, as well. But one of these is worth discussing further, as its impact on your health, body shape, performance and well-being is hard to overemphasize, and that's *nutrition*.

Science has finally caught up with nutrition and we know that you really *are* what you eat. Your body entirely replaces itself every two years. Your brain rebuilds itself in one year, your DNA renews itself every two months,

> **LISTEN:**
>
> *Mark Sisson Podcast*
>
> **TOPIC:**
> *Getting Fit*
>
> **URL and LINK:**
> *See page 206*

your blood is entirely renewed every four months, and your body builds a whole new skeleton every three months. In just one year, your body is 98% replaced. New building blocks are brought in and old ones are flushed out. Obviously this is a very complex process and having the right ingredients in place is essential.

Many modern foods are flat out toxic to our bodies and we now understand the biochemistry that makes them so. Sugars are inflammatory, their chemical nature makes them attack the lining of our blood vessels like water corrodes iron, and living with daily low-levels of inflammation leads to joint pain, low energy, circulatory problems, poor skin, and weight gain, too.

Sugars are added to an astonishing number of the foods we eat as companies exploit our innate attraction to sugars. We find it added to spaghetti sauce and tortillas, so-called healthy yogurts, and added to spicy hummus as well as our gourmet morning coffee. Once you begin reading package labels, it's astonishing how hard it is to avoid refined sugars. Our strongest recommendation is to abandon the USDA guidelines, which are overly weighted towards carbohydrates, and avoid nearly everything found in the center aisles of your local grocery store in favor of healthy, living food. The heavily processed foods found in the center aisles are loaded with fructose and stripped of life. Sure, there are calories to be found there, but not much else.

You are what you eat, and it took your authors a number of decades and their own chronic health issues to finally figure that out.

For Chris, an emerging path for gaining control over his nutritional health was *functional medicine*. After he had dropped the 30 pounds of excess weight, he was still plagued by various ailments with the worst two symptoms being achy joints and fatigue. *"Oh well,"* he thought, *"that's just age."*

When the pain and tiredness persisted he decided to go further and visit Dr. Aviva Wertkin (www.naturaemedical.com), a Naturopath and functional medicine specialist. Ten vials of blood, saliva and stool samples, and dozens of individual tests later, the results came back and conclusively showed that Chris had a leaky gut. His body was mounting a steady, low-level attack on 'invaders,' which turned out to be some of his favorite foods. Further, his adrenals were simply not functioning well and needed some support.

The food sensitivity test he took was perhaps the most transformative, as it showed which specific foods his body had been producing antibodies against and in what quantities. Dairy was out, especially eggs (the worst!...

and also one of his favorites), pecans were good but almonds were not. Meat and veggies were perfectly fine, but gluten was a problem. Clams were fine but scallops were terrible.

Instead of just getting older (although that's part of the story) what was happening was Chris was chronically inflamed, hence the low energy and joint pains. His narrative of 'getting older' turned out not to be entirely correct, or even the largest part of that story. The type-testing and guidance necessary to understand and treat Chris's 'condition' would have eluded most of the mainstream medical establishment. Believe it or not, nutrition training in medical schools is inadequate at best and completely missing, at worst.

Out of all of this inquiry emerged a startling observation: Chris's Western diet had been slowly harming him, and he ate a far better and healthier diet than most. Adjusting his eating patterns to the new regime (eat this but not *that*) resulted in quick improvements to his overall health and energy levels.

From all of this, a highly specific regimen of vitamins (he was super low in B12) and supplements was prescribed and his eating regime was tailored to exclude the specific trouble foods. After just three months, his joints began to ache less and within six months his vigor and health were getting back to normal.

There are two points here. First, a lot of what we eat is simply not good for us. The food pyramid is misguided at best, harmful at worst. Food companies exist to sell you food, not health or healthy food. They know that plenty of sugar does the trick and the explosion of obesity in the United States (and elsewhere in the world) reveals the extent of their success in slipping unhealthy (but craved) substances into your food.

Second, gathering the right information to make informed decisions about your eating habits is both easy and not very expensive.

Functional medicine offers the best approach we feel because it combines reams of solid medical data resulting from a wide assortment of modern testing with better nutritional information that most medical practitioners either ignore or simply don't know about. We're learning lots all the time about the ways in which our bodies interact with food, and especially our gut biomes, long ignored but suddenly at the forefront of a lot of exciting research.

To really dive into this area, we highly recommend that you investigate the works of Robb Wolf (robbwolf.com) who writes and speaks extensively on Paleo and anti-inflammatory diets and Chris Kresser (chriskresser.com), the *New York Times* bestselling author of the book *9 Steps to Perfect Health*, and functional medicine specialist.

LISTEN:

Robb Wolf
Podcast

TOPIC:
Good Nutrition

URL and LINK:
See page 206

LISTEN:

Chris Kresser
Podcast

TOPIC:
Functional Health

URL and LINK:
See page 206

Both have helped advance our understanding of the importance of nutrition, better sleep, and healthy exercise in our lives.

Going by the 80/20 rule, however, you will benefit enormously if you simply cut out the bad foods and eat more of the good foods in your life. For us that means lots of meat and veggies, a lot fewer carbs, and keeping sugar out of the diet as much as possible.

THE PRINCIPLES OF PERMACULTURE

The 8 Forms of Capital framework this book uses is based on the design principles of permaculture. And no form is more closely connected to permacuture than Living Capital. So it's worth taking a moment here to address the question: *What is permaculture, exactly?*

It comes from the combination of two words, permanent and agriculture (hence *perma*culture), and is the brainchild of Bill Mollison who created the idea in the 1970s. Deeply upset by the destruction of the natural ecosystems he studied, he turned to nature for ideas on how we could, and should, be doing things differently.

Natural systems, Mollison observed, are sustainable, providing for their own energy needs and recycling their own wastes. Left to its own devices, nature uses everything. There's no such thing as "waste" and every creature and system has a role to play.

Out of these observations came the core tenets of permaculture. The first is that the problem contains the solution. Another is to let nature do all of the work, whenever possible.

In the 1970s, Mollison and his student David Holmgren published several books explaining the principles of permaculture, and by the 1990s the practice had spread throughout the United States. Now it's worldwide, although still principally as a grassroots movement outside of the halls of traditional academia (for now).

To give a concrete example: Permaculture proposes planting 'dynamic accumulators' to complement your garden or orchard. Dynamic accumulators are plants that concentrate macronutrients from deep in the ground into their roots, stems and leaves, thereby replenishing these nutrients in the upper topsoil level. Planting accumulators such as clovers or vetches around your fruit trees is a great way to keep nitrogen levels up where the trees need them, without having to buy and add soil amendments yourself.

As another example, the first of the 12 permaculture design principles is "observe and interact." A permaculturally-minded gentleman with abundant Chinese chestnut trees was losing all of his nuts to squirrels. The traditional approach to this problem would have been to shoot the squirrels, but they have a breeding program designed to outlast any pellet gun on the market. The 'kill them' approach would have required oodles of time, and would end in defeat someday no matter how persistent the shooter.

The other pesky problem with Chinese chestnuts is that they're contained within a hard, wickedly spiked hull which looks like a medieval mace as much as anything. Stripping them off is time-consuming and occasionally painful. However, by observing for a while, this man with the squirrel "problem" noticed something. The squirrels would carefully and expertly strip off the spiky hull without damaging the nut and then go bury the nut somewhere nearby in soft earth. Thinking on this a bit, his solution was to sink five-gallon buckets full of sand near the chestnut trees.

LISTEN:

*Toby Hemenway
Podcast*

TOPIC:
Permaculture 101

URL and LINK:
See page 206

The squirrels, preferring this soft and convenient sand, would dutifully bury all the stripped chestnuts right in the buckets. For the man, harvesting the perfectly hulled nuts was as easy as running his fingers through soft sand. The problem (squirrels) contained the solution. No more problem, *and* less work to boot. As an addendum, he also put a piece of corn in the place of each removed chestnut so that the squirrels would not detect that their hiding spot was compromised and would therefore continue with the tradition.

INTERACT:

Peak Prosperity's Agricultural/ Permaculture Group

TOPIC:
Learn How to Grow Anything

URL and LINK:
See page 206

STEWARDING NATURE

Permaculture encourages us to be in harmony with nature wherever possible, allowing natural systems to do the work we want done. So learning how these systems work and how to best leverage them is an important part of the learning curve in developing your Living Capital.

Both Chris and Adam relocated to rural areas in order to learn how to use these re-generative practices to provide for their families. We put in gardens, orchards, apiaries, and livestock pens. We'll be honest; it takes years and a lot of mistakes before you get good at it. But the rewards are well worth it. Not only are we more self-sufficient as a result, but we also eat healthier, enjoy our time outside, are proud of our accomplishments, and love being surrounded by natural beauty.

However, you don't have to move to the country to gain many of the same benefits as we did. Even if you live in a city and have no access to a plot of land through a community garden, you can still grow herbs and some vegetables in pots on a windowsill or balcony. We highly recommend that you do this because reforming your connection to soil and growing at least *some* of the food you put in your mouth is a very powerful thing to do. It has effects well beyond the minor dollar value of the produced food.

For those with the ability to grow more, we highly recommend that, too. There's a night and day difference between producing 0% of your food and even just 3%. In a pinch, quickly ramping up from 3% to something far higher is possible—there's a lot of Knowledge, Living and Material Capital invested in that first 3%. But starting from 0% is an improbable and maybe even impossible task.

Transforming Your Land

When Chris bought his homestead in November 2009, it was a typical suburban house on a two-acre lot. Nothing fancy.

The spring of 2010 saw the building of a large outbuilding (20x40, two-story), the planting of an orchard, and the beginning of the installation of the garden plot. The orchard and garden were fenced to keep out deer and rabbits—although something surprising emerged when they had the fence holes drilled…pure sand came out of the holes.

It turns out the property rested on an ancient beachfront from when the ice-dammed lake Hitchcock dominated the region 10,000 years ago. The soil was mostly pure sand down to 62 feet.

Sand is nice and easy on plant roots and they love the well-drained part of the equation, but sandy soil—let alone pure sand!—cannot hold water or nutrients and that's a problem for gardeners.

The solution was to purchase topsoil, which was layered on the garden beds in a style known as 'lasagna gardening' because it consists of simply building up layers one on top of the other.

The best part of lasagna gardening is that it's easy. Cardboard is simply laid on top of the existing grass—no tilling!—which both preserves the existing soil structure and saves a lot of effort. Other layers include compost, shredded maple leaves in the fall, and every scrap of grass from mowing the lawn.

Other main improvements include putting heavy landscape fabric down under the walkways which eliminates weeding, and installing drip irrigation which cuts the human involvement for watering from hours to mere seconds. Just turn on the water, go to sleep, and in the morning the entire garden is watered perfectly and deeply. Lawn mowing cuttings are used to mulch extensively around the planting cutting down on weeds.

No weeds and no weeding!

Between all of these improvements, managing the garden takes just a few minutes a day after the initial spring planting. Weeding is barely a job anymore, and the main 'chore' is picking fresh vegetables and finding new ways to prepare them.

Similarly, planting an orchard in 2010 involved a bit of planning, a community 'planting day' where lots of people came to learn and to assist, and now, the tree trunks which were only as thick as a thumb on planting

day, are too large to get two hands around in 2015. As of the writing of this book, the branches are bending with fruit.

To really improve the property yield, chickens live in the same fenced enclosure and a wide variety of understory plants are encouraged to mimic natural diversity. That's courtesy of permaculture thinking which usually involves greater plant varieties, stacked layers, and stacked functions (where one plant's waste becomes the next plant's food).

Bees are kept in hives on the property and love the orchard blossoms. Everyone benefits from being in living relationship with each other. We get fruit, the bees get food year round, we get honey, the trees get well fertilized and we get eggs. Okay, maybe we get a bit more out of the deal.

THE CHOICE IS OURS

Developing Living Capital is quite involved. It's often a bit overwhelming for folks who have never grown a garden, and feel pressured suddenly to become full-scale farmers and ranchers. That's not the message here at all.

But there is a fair amount to learn for those who want to improve their health, learn the skills to grow *some* of their own food, or just live in better balance with nature. Which is why we've created a number of resources at PeakProsperity.com that will help you get up the learning curve, and tap the expertise of our community, which has experts in aquaculture, greenhouse production, animal husbandry, and other skills.

Moreover, we highly encourage you to **support local farmers who farm the right way,** in balance and sustainably. The more demand we can create for locally grown foods that also support greater local Living Capital; the better off we will all be individually and collectively.

So even if you do not want to have a garden, or cannot have one, you can build up local Living Capital by supporting those farmers who share your passion for living soils and living systems. Put your money to good use by spending it with those who are acting responsibly and regneratively.

In closing, the only hope we have of having a future worth living is if we adopt new behaviors on a wide scale right now. Instead of treating the natural world as if it were a stranger's house to trash during a party, we need to become more

---

INTERACT:

Peak Prosperity's Groups

TOPIC:
Connect with
Like-Minded People

URL and LINK:
See page 206

careful and thoughtful stewards of the planetary home in which we all live. With our intelligence directed in positive ways, we can speed up and enhance nature's abundance many times over.

If we don't, nature will take care of our excesses for us, but probably not in ways we will enjoy. As biologist Guy McPherson warns: *Nature bats last.*

Given the time it takes to develop, start now on your investments in Living Capital. If the time arrives when you need to count on your health or your ability to source a portion of your own food calories, if you don't already have those in place, it will be years too late to start.

CHAPTER 8

MATERIAL CAPITAL

Material Capital consists of the tangible things that meet our needs, infuse our lives with beauty, that we can see and touch and which either provide value to us or insulate us from future costs. Things like buildings, roads, art, fences, bridges, power facilities, factories, cars, wells, and tractors.

On our own properties, this includes things like solar hot water and PV systems, generators, honey extractors, back-up heating and water systems, and hand tools—the list goes on.

This topic could fill an entire book on its own. In this chapter, we'll provide guidance on how to develop the foundational aspects of Material Capital, and leave the detailed recommendations (such as specific products to consider) for the *What Should I Do?* companion workbook to this publication.

Trading money for "stuff" is easy, and very familiar to those of us living in a consumer culture. Which is why after taking steps to safeguard their money, most people focus next on acquiring Material Capital in their resilience-building efforts.

TRUE WEALTH

We've all been conditioned (marketed to) to think of wealth solely in terms of money, or more accurately, the digital ones and zeros that represent our personal financial holdings within the financial system that have mainly been sent off to Wall Street for "safe keeping." But money is not actually wealth. It's a *claim* on wealth.

Money has no meaning and no value if you can't buy something with it. Imagine having a huge pile of $100 bills, a billion dollars worth, on a pallet. Now imagine you and that pallet of money are in the middle of the Sahara Desert and there's nobody around, not even a nomad on a camel, within 100 miles.

What value does all that cash have for you then? It may be good fuel for a signal fire perhaps, but that's about it. That is, the tangible resources you could use to rescue yourself—water, food, clothes, a dune buggy and 50 gallons of fuel—would be real forms of wealth in that situation. And you'd gladly buy them with your pile of paper, er *money*, if you could.

What we want to reinforce here is that *real* wealth comes in three forms:

1. **Primary wealth** is things like rich soils, thick stands of trees, clear and abundant water, mineral ores, and oil in the ground.

2. **Secondary wealth** results from transforming primary wealth into tangible goods people want: lumber, food, steel, and gasoline. Secondary wealth, then, also includes the means of production for these goods (factories, plant and equipment, etc.).

3. **Tertiary wealth** is what many of us are most familiar with. It's simply all of the paper claims placed on primary and secondary wealth: stocks, bonds, derivatives—and our money. We've been told our entire lives that these represent wealth, despite being nothing more than mere claims. And history has a way of violating and reducing those claims, sometimes all the way to zero. It's then that people remember what 'true wealth'—which we define as the primary and secondary forms—actually is.

This is why Material Capital is so important. It represents one of the more obvious ways to convert some, or perhaps *a lot*, of your financial (tertiary) wealth into primary and secondary wealth. For example, you can exchange money for arable acreage, energy production systems or productive enterprises.

We consider many of these purchases as *investments*, in many ways superior in return to what Wall Street can offer. Some will behave like insurance policies, some like securities that return positive future cash flows, and some will reduce your future expenses, while others will add beauty, enjoyment and utility to your life.

Pursuing Material Capital is really an invitation to stretch your concept of 'investment' away from the single-minded and narrow definition that financial marketers have lavishly advertised. Invest in yourself instead of sending your money off to enrich the Wall Street casino, and praying you get back more than you forked over. Instead, invest in beauty, comfort, and reduced future expenses, as well as ways to increase future cash flows.

USEFUL PERSPECTIVE

Cry Once

Have you ever noticed that yard sales and flea markets are filled with the same two types of "stuff"? There you will find decades-old tools and appliances that still work, as well as newer crap that doesn't. The newer stuff is usually made out of cheap plastics and has been manufactured by the most inexpensive labor available at the time. And the old products, made with much more care and better materials, amazingly still have useful years left in them.

There's an important lesson to be learned here.

When acquiring Material Capital, go for the highest quality you can afford. One of our longtime readers at Peak Prosperity, who knows the value of dependability from his years of wilderness and military training, has coined this the *"cry once"* philosophy.

Generally, the higher the quality of an item, the higher its purchase price. It can hurt to pay top dollar, hence the "cry" part. But our own experience confirms that if you consistently buy cheaper items, which usually means at lower quality, you tend to cry more due to inferior usefulness, poor design, aggravating break downs, and shorter life span.

Over many years of observation, we've calculated that it is much less costly in the long run to "cry once" and invest in well-designed, durable products. Once the initial tears dry, you won't have any further regrets

This strategy applies to nearly everything, from goods to services to relationships. Invest in quality to ensure they'll be there when you need to count on them most.

This is especially important given a future defined by the Three Es. If you decide to buy cheap, what's to guarantee replacement parts will still be available later on?

So *cry once.*

Simple Is Better

Another recommendation we have is to prefer simple solutions over complex ones.

For example, for those looking to install a hand pump on your property well, we love the Simple Pump, which has a bare minimum of moving parts yet can push water, under pressure, into your house from as much as 250 feet below ground level. There's not a lot to break. And if any part does, it's simple enough to be locally fashioned or sourced.

Our advice also means avoid buying things that try to be too many things at once.

Recently a wildly-successful kickstarter campaign raised over $13 million dollars from over 60,000 backers for a new type of beverage cooler. Yes, a cooler—like the sort you bring to the beach. Why were people so excited? Because this cooler does *everything*.

It's a cooler; but it also has a USB power outlet, an integrated 18V blender, and a powered outdoor bluetooth speaker. There's even a flashlight built right into the lid. With all of these features (there are even more we didn't list) this cooler is trying to be a lot of things. Too many things, in our opinion.

As engineers will tell you, mixing functions almost always results in lower performance and more things to break. For instance, this product's batteries give off heat when charging, and heat is not something you generally want in a cooler. At least that's how we see it. As we said, mixed functions deliver lower performance.

Which is why we suggest that you avoid unnecessary complexity wherever possible in your Material Capital purchases. While they might seem sexy and fun in the showroom, they aren't what you want in a pinch when they absolutely *have* to work.

Think three Rs: rugged, robust, and repairable.

Or just think *simple*.

Buy Happiness (Or at Least, Satisfaction)

Next, we think you should buy things that add to the quality of your life, that give you joy every time you use them. You probably already have a few such things in your life—a favorite pair of boots, the car you really love, the piece of art that never fails to please when you look at it.

While increasing Material Capital is often about buying more stuff it's important to realize it not about materialism. It's about *value*. Primarily functional value, but it should also include aesthetic value, too.

As you decide what to procure, make your decision based on what you assess you need in your life, as well as what you'd really like to have. The two aren't always as mutually exclusive as people imagine. If you deem you need a way to heat your house without fossil fuels, and you really like the aesthetic appeal of a masonry heater versus a wood stove, then go with that.

That way, no matter which future arrives, you'll be warm in the winter, be less dependent on fossil energy, and be pleased on a daily basis when you use, or even walk past, the masonry heater.

The purpose of life is not just to endure, but to *enjoy*. Wherever we can, we strive to surround ourselves with function and beauty, and it's not especially difficult to do. If the Three Es turn out not to have the impact we predict, hey, no problem. We'll have lived a life that has pleased us, surrounded by things that bring us happiness. And if the future indeed proves disruptive? Boy, are we sure glad we invested in our Material Capital early on.

So buy with an eye to enhancing your quality of life.

WHEN TO START

When is the right time to begin? Right now, of course! *Now* is the right time.

Preparing before a crisis hits is responsible. But afterwards, as mentioned, preparing is not only much harder, but potentially irresponsible if it slips over into the realm of hoarding.

The good news is that today you can click your computer mouse and have your desired items dropped off in your driveway two days later. This is one of the more profound miracles of plentiful petroleum, which will not last forever. Again, each of us should plan as if we don't know what tomorrow will bring.

Many of the things you may need will *take time* to identify and afford. Maybe lots of time. Installing a solar energy system, a garden, or re-insulating your house will take time to design and implement. There are lots of decisions to be made and only so many brain cells and thought cycles available. Remember, building resilience is a journey not a destination. It's just not possible to "finish" everything quickly. Chris and Adam's own efforts to increase their Material Capital have taken many years, and they are very much still ongoing.

WHERE TO INVEST

That's right, we consider appropriate material purchases to be *investments*. They have immediate and long-term returns, both financial and functional.

The three places to focus your attention are your community, commercially, and your homestead.

Community

In Chris' community, there are several material investments that have been shared among neighbors including a log splitter, a chicken plucker, a generator, and a honey extractor. Instead of each family having one of these for themselves, sharing these items is both cost effective and helpful for building Social Capital and tightening community bonds.

While bought by specific families, other families know about them and borrow them from time to time, creating additional opportunities for connection and trading. So the thought process here is to think about what your community needs and then see if you can provide anything to meet them. This could be equipment like a tractor, mowers, generators, pumps, solar ovens, or moveable electric fencing (surprisingly handy stuff).

While these resources add to the material capital on your own homestead, when loaned out, they become excellent community investments.

Further, you can consider making local loans and investments, a powerful way of increasing local Material Capital while supporting people and their dreams during important moments.

Commercial

Here you want to center on the two concepts of reducing future costs (outlays) and deepening inventories. For many businesses there's a balancing act between the two, but the idea here is to ask what would happen if any of the needed inputs to your business became scarce, expensive, or even impossible to source?

Keeping a lean inventory is cost effective, but it's not resilient. Too many decades of financialization have over-concentrated our attention on being cost-effective and it's time to reconsider the existing risks to our supply chains. For example, imagine a community that fully enjoys the low prices of a local Walmart, which, over time, has driven all the other competing stores out of business. Should the Walmart's China supply chain ever be severed for any reason, everyone will quite suddenly discover that the other side of "cost-effective" is "vulnerability" as the shelves go quickly bare.

The concept of "re-localization" so popular in the food movement, can and should be extended to local businesses, perhaps your own, if you have one. Shop local and buy products sourced as close to home as possible as an exercise (and investment) in local economy resilience.

Homestead

When Chris purchased his house and started building Material Capital, he found all sorts of ways to invest in solutions that would reduce future expenses, provide healthy, calculable returns, and improve his quality of life.

One exceptionally good example was the installation of a solar hot water system. There's nothing very fancy or high tech about such a system. It's not sexy and exciting like a Tesla model S. It's just a couple of hot water tanks, some piping, and a few black boxes on the roof that absorb the sun's heat.

The entire system cost around $8,800 after the tax credits. For years now, it's been quietly and dependably heating and storing 240 gallons of water to 165 degrees F using only a tiny 100-watt circulating pump.

Imagine using a single 100W light bulb to heat two giant home water tanks to a piping-hot 165 degrees and you get a sense of the energy gains involved. The sun does an absolutely brilliant job of heating things up.

Formerly, all of the hot water at his home was provided by an oil furnace. Now, the oil bill is 33% lower and the furnace does not even switch on from May to November. This represents a savings of approximately $1,000 per year (depending on oil prices) meaning the system will have an eight-year pay back period, give or take.

However, because the system has a 25-year life span, the return on this investment in strict dollar terms will be at least $25,000. That's a triple digit financial return compared to the system's cost of $8,800. Try getting that out of Wall Street, guaranteed. But that's just the monetary return.

Along the way no fossil fuels will be burned to heat the water that used to be heated by oil, and that feels good. Long showers feel better knowing the hot water is a product of the sun.

But in a future scenario where oil may not even be available or is vastly more expensive? Ah, then solar water heaters will become incredibly valuable if, like your authors, you consider hot water to be among the several things that make being a human worthwhile. Knowing that hot water will always be available is one of those back-of-the-mind liberating investments you can make.

With proper focus, you can find numerous other investments all around your property providing these same financial and functional return streams.

EMERGENCY PREPARATIONS

Everybody should have basic emergency preparations in their home, especially if you live in an area subject to natural disasters. Here's what we consider to be the bare minimum of basic emergency preparation supplies:

- One month of food (three months is better)
- Hand-cranked radio for communications
- Small solar charging device and rechargeable batteries
- Flashlights and small LED reading lamps that use the same rechargeable batteries as above

- Basic EMT medical kit
- Self-defense items ranging from better locks, a bigger dog, pepper spray and/or guns
- Cash to support you for three months out of the bank
- Gold and silver (insurance policy amounts)
- Storage containers for water and fuel
- Blankets/sleeping bags/warm clothes
- A deck of cards. (Or whatever board games you like to play because once the emergency has settled down and before life starts up again you're going to have lots of spare time.)

A much more detailed list with specific product recommendations are available in the *What Should I Do?* companion workbook.

THE BASIC MATERIAL PREPARATIONS

If you're just starting out, then there are some basic preparations that we recommend to everyone, regardless of age, means, or rural vs. urban status.

Food

Everyone should strive to store away at least three months' (but preferably six months') worth of emergency food. Buy it, put in in your basement or the next coolest location you can find, and forget about it. Hopefully you'll never need to use it, but you'll sure sleep better knowing you have it.

Storing this much food is easy to accomplish and pretty low-cost, especially when completed over the course of time.

We have an excellent and detailed Wiki at Peak Prosperity that covers this topic in extensive detail for those who want to go deeper:

READ:

Food Storage Made Easy

TOPIC:
Purchasing Food From Mormon Canneries

URL and LINK:
See page 206

http://www.peakprosperity.com/wiki/133/food-storage

But for those who want to take care of things in one fell swoop, our primary recommendation is that you use one of the numerous canneries run by the Church of Latter Day Saints. These facilities offer the most cost-effective and high quality solution of which we're aware. They're open to anyone, Mormons and non-Mormons alike (your authors are not Mormons and have used these services numerous times).

How much food should you buy for each person in your household? The same LDS service has a handy calculator available at **providentliving. com/preparedness/food-storage/foodcalc/**

Of course, if you have ravenous teenage boys in the house you may want to multiply their rations by two and divide grandma's in half. Similarly, if you're preparing for days of heavy work in the cold you'll have to add more daily calories than if you're planning on boring days of playing Monopoly® waiting for things to get back to normal.

So figure out what sort of future you'd like to prepare for and then adjust your food purchases accordingly. In actuality, it makes sense to store more food than you'll need for just your immediate family. There are certain to be members of your extended family or neighborhood who are not taking these precautions and will need support. Storing extra food in advance will work in both your best interests. Secondly, food may become a handy bargaining substance if things get rocky enough. It sure won't hurt to have a little extra on hand.

Chris, who lives up in a northern climate, has chosen to have eight months of food on hand to help make it from November to July—the lean months. (Fun fact: In historical Europe the month with the highest rate of starvation deaths was June, the last month before the earliest field crops started to produce.)

Another option is to buy freeze-dried food. You'll have a much wider selection of meals from which to choose and it keeps just as long. But it's expensive.

Alternatively, you can group together with others to place a bulk order to buy and pack your own long-term storage foods. In addition to the food itself, you'll also need to order the packing materials; buckets, Mylar liners, desiccants, oxygen absorbers, and a means of sealing the Mylar bags. While this approach is great for community building, we can tell you from experience, it's a much more complicated and expensive route to take. But if you have specific needs, such as gluten intolerance, this may be your only option.

No matter how you source your storage food, it needs to be stored well to last a long time. The main enemies of a long shelf life are oxygen, humidity, and heat. Vacuum seals and desiccants are the primary means for defending against the first two. As for heat, food needs to be stored under 70 degrees F to last for 20 to 30 years, but at or below 60 is even better. Generally speaking for every ten degrees above 70 you can knock off between five and 10 years of shelf life, depending on the food we're talking about.

READ:

Community Food Storage

TOPIC:
A How-To Guide for your Neighborhood

URL and LINK:
See page 207

The other part of the food plan is to keep a **deep pantry**. By this we mean that you simply buy more of everything you already eat until you have a pantry that is filled with about a year's worth of the boxes, cans, jars, and bottles of all the sauces, tuna, ketchup, and other foods you eat. This is another example of a smart practice no matter what the future holds. You're going to eat these things anyway, and with rising food prices all but guaranteed, buying more today actually saves you money over time.

A truly excellent guide on all things food storage related can be found here: **www.peakprosperity.com/wiki/133/food-storage**

So that's it for the food basics. Buy some long-term storage food, keep a deep pantry, and you'll be off to a great start.

Water
In extreme survival the "rule of 3" goes like this; you can survive:

- 3 minutes without air
- 3 hours without shelter
- 3 days without water
- 3 weeks without food

Okay, we're going to assume that in the future, whatever happens, air and shelter are available to you. With food also now taken care of, that leaves water.

Water is something that most people take for granted until it disappears. Then it becomes immediately obvious how essential it is for life. Farmers in California and residents of Sao Paolo, Brazil both learned tough lessons through their respective water shortages in 2014 and 2015. Once it dwindles, your life changes in a hurry.

The first and easiest part of securing your personal water supplies involves filtration and storage.

Having a good filtration solution will allow you to create drinkable water out of nearly any fresh water source.

For effectiveness, simplicity and durability, we use ceramic filtration systems like the Big Berkey water filter and its cousins.

All of them operate on the same principle: water is poured into an upper reservoir and gravity drags it down into the lower chamber through microporous ceramic 'candles' that have very fine pore diameters. These were used by the British army in India as they proved incredibly effective at filtering out and preventing water-borne diseases.

These are so effective you can filter a stagnant puddle from the roadway through them, or the most foul of pond water, and obtain water that is safe to drink. It may not smell as terrific as your current tap water, but it will be safe.

As long as you're able to access some source of water, you should be able to make it drinkable.

There are other filtrations solutions, usually used for camping, to be aware of. They're lightweight and travel easily with you, but are really only suited to filtering a quart or two at a time. You wouldn't want to be doing large scale cooking or cleaning with the water from these devices, it's just for drinking.

As for storing water, we recommend plastic five-gallon water totes, bricks, or carboys because these are easily portable from a water source back to your home or camp.

In 2014, Chris and his family experienced 10 weeks without water because their well failed and the so-called polar vortex had frozen the ground so hard that it was impossible to repair. How did they survive for those 10 weeks? By toting eight, five-gallon water totes back and forth from the neighbor's house. These 40 gallons lasted for an average of two and a half days, supplying everything from flushing and dish washing water, to drinking water, to shower water. Without ready water storage totes on hand, the whole affair would have been far more difficult to manage.

Larger solutions include above ground storage tanks, underground cisterns, and rain catchment systems. These especially make sense in the drier areas of the country.

A single inch of rain on 1,000 feet of catchment area results in 600 gallons of stored water. A typical home with a 40x50 foot dimension will therefore have the potential to capture 1,200 gallons for every inch of rain. Live in an area with only 10 inches of rain a year? That's okay; you can still capture 12,000 gallons of water a year.

Those with wells should consider installing a hand pump (like the Simple Pump we mentioned at the start of this chapter) as backup in case of well-pump failure. Surprisingly, a bottom-draw hand pump can push water up from 250 feet down. These can be installed in the same well shaft as a typical well to operate in parallel with the already installed electric pump.

The summary here is that there are lots of ways to supply yourself with water, but the details depend a lot on where you live. For anyone, however, having a water filter on hand makes sense. How much water storage or tote capability you select is up to you, and obviously where you live will have a big impact on what you choose to do. Adam lives in California, currently under a very serious drought in 2015 with hot temperatures, while Chris lives in Massachusetts, currently having a very wet and cool summer.

Both have multiple means for filtering and storing water (remember redundancy!) and would replace them as quickly as possible if they happened to be lost or damaged.

Energy

Once food and water are dealt with, energy is the next big area to focus on. If you own a home, we highly recommend undertaking a basic energy audit. Once that's complete, start targeting the highest-return investments you can make in increasing your home's energy efficiency. After that, look at the range of home energy production options and determine which may be appropriate for you.

The goal here is to become as energy independent as possible. From fossil fuels, and from monolithic utility companies.

The range of efficiency and production solutions is so vast that covering it all here just isn't feasible. But we have an excellent primer at the PeakProsperity.com website that walks you through all of the most common options and their projected returns on investment:

http://www.peakprosperity.com/wiki/75/home-energy

Home energy investments generally have excellent returns. Insulation can have a 15% to 18% return on investment for the average home. Solar hot water, as we discussed earlier, can pay for itself in just eight years but last for 25 years making the rate of return well over 100% while delivering the comfort of knowing that as long as the sun shines you can have hot water.

Solar PV, an increasingly cost-effective and turnkey solution, also has excellent returns, although those will be reduced heavily for US residents if the solar federal tax credit is not extended when it expires in 2016.

However, the really big benefits of having alternative energy supplies is the redundancy you receive between your system and the electricity grid. If one is lost, you still have the other.

Given that foreign hackers were found in 2013 to have gained malicious root access to the US electricity grid and that an electromagnetic pulse from a massive solar storm just narrowly missed the earth in 2012—both of which could have crippled electrical power across America—having redundant systems makes a lot of sense for those who can afford it.

If you can get this insurance, plus do it cost effectively, get a good financial return on your money, and lighten your carbon footprint, why *wouldn't* you do this?

LISTEN:	LISTEN:
NASA Podcast	James Woolsey Podcast
TOPIC: The Dangers of Coronal Mass Ejections	TOPIC: The Vulnerability of our Electrical Grid
URL and LINK: See page 207	URL and LINK: See page 207

SUMMARY

There are numerous other categories of Material Capital important to resilience. Tools, machines, communications devices, transportation, and first aid supplies—just to list a few.

As mentioned, the accompanying *What Should I Do Guide?* provides much more specifics around products to consider, as well as step-by-step guidance based on your personal resilience goals.

In closing, here's an inspiring personal story from one of Peak Prosperity's community members, who is building a better life for himself through his investments in Material Capital:

> Though I did not want to accept the inevitable conclusion, I realized that our beautiful home in the suburbs and our weekend home nearby in the mountains at a ski resort would not provide a safe, independent and sustainable location.
>
> We needed a farm. But not your typical, isolated farm. Instead, we needed a good balance between privacy and neighbors nearby for support structure and mutual security. In a future of diminished travel and resources, it will take more than just a few friends or family members to provide needed skills and manpower—it really does take a village.
>
> At first, my property search took me to remote locations. My wife quickly changed that. She informed me that we were not going to live in some isolated cave, waiting for something bad that might never happen.
>
> She correctly determined that we should continue be able to enjoy all the luxuries and conveniences that our modern society has to offer. Her criteria was that she wanted to be within a 30-minute drive of a town that offered excellent medical care, culture, restaurants, grocery stores, movie theaters, and shopping.
>
> We found our solution at Bundoran Farm—a 2,300-acre preservation development of 99 residential lots built around an existing farm operation with cattle, a vineyard and winery, and a 165-acre apple orchard.
>
> We acquired an entire section of the property consisting of 12 lots, sold two to my business partner, and consolidated three to keep for ourselves. As a national authority on community associations, my fellow owners elected me as their representative to the developer-controlled board of directors.
>
> More than a year was devoted to designing the home, the barn and the gardens. The house and barn are unusual in that the core of the exterior walls are concrete and steel, the framing is steel, the roof is metal, and all exterior trim is PVC—but you would never know from looking at them. Both structures look traditional.
>
> After constructing a road to the site, I first built the barn so that it could also be used as a staging area for materials during construction of the house. The barn faces due south, and I installed 42 photovoltaic panels on the barn roof that produce an

average of 10.3 kilowatts of power. The PV panels are currently grid-tied, but will soon be augmented with additional PV panels and rerouted to a battery-storage bank inside the house.

The exterior walls of the house are massive, energy-efficient Insulated Concrete Forms, and the underside of the roof is super-insulated with 5" of sprayed closed-cell foam. Heating and cooling is produced from two geothermal heat pumps, and almost all of the lights are energy-efficient LEDs. Of course, we have our own well and septic field, and are installing cisterns to capture rainwater from the barn and house, as well as an emergency cistern located further up the mountain.

Clearly this gentleman and his family have made huge strides in expanding their Material Capital. It's truly impressive to see the level of planning and dedication that these people, and those like them, are bringing to the world.

While the efforts of the rest of us are likely to be more modest, it's important to know that there are others preparing as we are. Likely more than we realize. From the interactions we have through our work at Peak Prosperity, we see that an increasing number of people, especially highly successful people who study the economy carefully, have come to the conclusion that serious changes are on the way and that the time to redirect their finances and time towards material capital has come.

CHAPTER 9

KNOWLEDGE CAPITAL

Many people tend to view the act of preparing for an uncertain future as the accumulation of physical "things" that will offer protection or provide some degree of advantage. Food storage, solar panels, home security systems, gold and silver, even communities of people—these sorts of things.

But focusing on just the "stuff" is missing the full picture. Tangible assets can unexpectedly lose value, break, get lost or stolen, or otherwise not come through for you when it matters most. How will you repair or replace them? If you can't do either, what will you fall back on?

Here's where we introduce the concept of Knowledge Capital: the "stuff" inside your head. This is comprised of *what you know* (information and intellectual models) and *what you know how to do* (experience). We typically go to school to acquire the former and develop the latter through hours of real-world application, usually in the workplace.

KNOWLEDGE CAPITAL IS NECESSARY TO CREATE **VALUE**

Knowledge Capital really comes alive with the marriage of theory and practice. The degree of overlap between the two is important because it determines your level of *Mastery*. And mastery is important because it's what you use to create *Value*. The more mastery you have, the more value you can create to exchange for other desired resources (income, goods, services, etc.) or to enjoy directly yourself (entertainment, homestead improvements, social currency, etc.).

As mentioned, mastery lives at the intersection between the Information and Intellectual Models we use and the Experience that comes with putting them into practice:

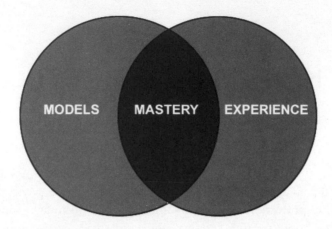

And that overlap, that Mastery, is what we use to improve our circumstances. By using it to build things, make systems more efficient, design better solutions—a myriad of different methods—we bring Value to the world around us.

For the more empirically-minded, think of this relationship as a set of equations:

$$\textbf{Information + Application = Mastery}$$

and

$$\textbf{Mastery x (Effort/Time) = Value}$$

So, in order to produce Value, you need to start with Information and Application. And you need to have both—they're equally important. Information without Application is practically useless. Things hardly ever run in the real world in the same way they're predicted on the chalkboard—something all those early aeronauts who crashed before the Wright brothers' successful flight at Kitty Hawk learned the hard way.

Not only can pure "book smarts" be useless, it can be dangerous. The hubris of those who think they understand everything but don't have an on-the-ground perspective to counterbalance their judgment often leads to perfect logic that crumples when it slams into an imperfect reality. The current efforts of the Federal Reserve to sidestep the business cycle and manage the prices of all assets around the world using only the crude pairing of interest rates and the printing press is just one such example.

Application uninformed by Information is equally futile. It's just blindly going through the motions without understanding the why or the how of it. Imagine the unskilled worker whose job is to pull a lever on his machine to complete a task. What if he needs the machine to increase output? What will he do if the machine stops? Or the lever breaks? Our worker is helpless to address questions like these outside of his rote experience. Such blind adherence to "it's always been done this way" can be seen in our modern "Big Ag" factory-farming practices. They deplete our topsoils and require expensive and unhealthy inputs annually, ignoring the well-spring of new models demonstrating a better way to affordably farm the same foods organically and much more sustainably.

So, here's a great question: if the combination of Information and Application—what we call Mastery—is so important to creating Value, why aren't we encouraged and trained to pursue it from a young age?

A Broken System, A Broken Narrative

The answer is a sad one, like so many that have led to our current set of predicaments.

Bad Models

The modern educational system in the developed world has its roots in eighteenth-century Prussia. A model for compulsory primary schooling was decreed by Frederick II, the third Hohenzollern king of Prussia and renowned military strategist. His framework provided for free but mandatory education for the populace, the state construction of schools, teacher funding, and a structured curriculum—elements that continue to serve as the foundation for national education systems worldwide today.

Not surprisingly, the military structure of top-down teacher authority and student compliance resonated with civic leaders during the Industrial Revolution. Horace Mann brought the Prussian schooling model to America in the mid-1800s, and what resulted was the modern one teacher, 28 students, in an 800-square-foot classroom approach that persists today. The original military-model morphed into a factory-model of teaching, designed to prepare American youth for the newly industrialized economy they would enter. This factory approach was, not surprisingly, designed to produce good factory workers.

Such a model, focused on rote memorization and conformity, leaves little room for creative thought and exploration. Nor does it connect to the importance of discovering how "book learning" actually plays out in practice in the real world. Students are praised for regurgitating facts, and punished for errors. Remember our praise of mistakes in Chapter 6 on developing resilience? Our current education system vilifies mistakes, using low grades and social shaming to penalize those who attempt to think outside the box.

As a result, we have an educational system that actually prohibits the development of Mastery. And it does so not only in terms of its approach, but in its affordability, as well.

The cost of higher education has grown leaps and bounds faster than the cost of living over the past four decades (over 1,000% since the late 1970s!) and it's important to understand why:

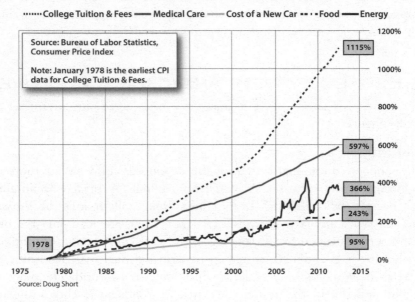

Inflation Comparison: Percent Growth

in earlier chapters, our modern economy is addicted to constant growth in outstanding credit. Naturally, the big-ticket purchases that consumers make—most commonly housing and education—are the ones most funded by credit, and so the system does its best to make it as easy as possible for folks to get into those loans. In the case of college loans, students have historically borrowed from private banks and the U.S. government (through programs like Ford and Perkins loans).

Notice here that the colleges and universities themselves aren't issuing loans to students. This means that they don't have any exposure to their alumni's ability or inability to repay their loans. Any costs of loan default are born by the lender, not the college.

This important observation explains the perverse incentive that educational institutions have: *to raise their fees as high as the market will possibly bear.* Each additional dollar their matriculating students are willing to borrow is pure profit for them. Especially if colleges can get away with diluting quality costs, which many are, behind an ivy-laced smokescreen of venerability.

So, it's little surprise that tuition and fees have risen. But there's more to the story.

Globalization has led to rising incomes across the developing world. In countries like China and India, where education is highly valued as the essential ingredient to success in life, millions of millionaires have been minted who want the best schooling for their children. There is now tremendous competition for spots at American universities, largely driven by the influx of foreign students, many of whom can afford to pay for their tuition in full.

Add to this the weak job market that has persisted since the 2008 crisis. The unemployment rate for recent college graduates remains twice as high as that for the average U.S. adult. Because the level and brand of their education is one of the only dimensions these younger workers can use to compete in the job market, they'll sign any loan agreement in order to get a "good" degree.

What many don't realize, until it's too late, is that the value of the degree they receive is increasingly worth nowhere near as much as the price they paid to get it.

Students are graduating with crushing student loan balances that will make them debt-serfs for most of their lives (and that's assuming they're able to earn the average income). How bad is it? Over 40 million Americans now collectively owe over $1.3 trillion in student debt. Debt, mind you, that isn't dismissible by declaring personal bankruptcy (which even gambling debts are!).

And all for what? A paper diploma that rarely is accompanied by any practical know-how. Graduating students may have a fair amount of "book learning" (if they didn't get too distracted by the four-year party-fest that college has turned into for many), but they don't really know how to "do" much of anything at all at this stage. Is it really that surprising that the unemployment rate for recent grads is so high? Or that the jobs they do get are often unskilled and low-pay?

Is that an outcome worth becoming a lifelong debt serf for?

No, it's not.

Bad Information

Another corrupting factor in play here is the influence our culture's narrative has.

From a very young age, the media is setting false priorities for us. It sells the idea of wealth as fame and fortune. We are taught to idolize celebrities and to aspire to their flamboyant spendthrift lifestyles. Our economy trains us to think of ourselves as "consumers," and our politicians push us to "go shopping more" as a patriotic duty. From the Kardashians to Silicon Valley gazillionaires to the Wall Street elite—we're told/sold that happiness and meaning is measured in money. And the more you have, and the more you can spend on vain trophy assets, the more you're winning the game of life.

This obsession with the top 1% is a fool's errand.

First off, it's based on the false premise that money = fulfillment. As we wrote about at length in Chapter 6 on Financial Capital, it simply doesn't.

Second, these unrealistic expectations set by society take a destructive emotional toll. Even though basic mathematics tell us that, by definition, 99% of us aren't in the top 1%, our cultural programming tells us that we *should* be. The result? A deep unhappiness with our reality. Feelings of personal failure, being cheated by fate, of envy at what others have. It's this toxic soup of disappointments that leads folks into depression, reckless spending habits, self-medication or social withdrawal.

And it's this same narrative that drives so many to pursue a degree from a "good" school so they can get a "good" job in order to earn a "good" paycheck. Those considering following a different course are pressured, cautioned and heckled that they're "throwing their lives away" by risking a break from the herd.

As data-driven analysts, we know empirically that bad information and bad models lead to bad decisions. And bad decisions lead to bad outcomes.

So, given the brokenness of our educational system and our cultural narrative, what outcomes do we end up with? Millions of graduates who pursue careers for money rather than personal fulfillment. Often becoming dangerously indebted in the process, and the eventual outcome is predictable. Whether it takes five years or 15, the vast majority of these workers wake up to realize at some point that they've gone down a professional path they regret.

Their work has little meaning for them, and yet they feel trapped, unable to escape from it. Deloitte's Shift Index survey reports that 80% of workers report they are dissatisfied with their jobs. Similarly, Gallup reports that 72% of employees are 'disengaged' from their work due to lack of interest or conflicting values. But due to fears of lacking expertise, or of inability to pay their mortgage/school loans/life expenses, most can't find the courage to deal with the risks of making a transition, and simply trudge along, resigned to a career shackled to the rat-race wheel.

Pursuing Mastery

So, how you can rise above the challenges? By pursing Mastery. Specifically, the *right* kind of Mastery.

And what kind is the right kind? Whatever Mastery needed to create the type of life you want to live. This is different for each of us, and depends on our passions, aptitudes and goals.

As a refresher, Mastery is the combination of "what you know" and "what you know how to do." It's the knowledge you apply to create Value, which you will in turn exchange for other forms of capital that will make you more resilient. That capital may be financial, like money received for a good or service delivered. It may be Living or Material, if you barter your services in exchange for food or other assets. Or it could be Social, such as when you perform a favor for someone (e.g., helping a neighbor with his tax preparation) who is then in turn more likely to reciprocate if you ever need assistance with anything.

As the path to Mastery is specific to the individual, how does one go about it?

Through the following process, which is provided in much more specific detail in our book *Finding Your Way To Your Authentic Career.*

The fundamental steps of the process are as follows:

Self-Assessment

Start with an honest assessment of the intellectual learning and practical expertise you possess today. Given past fields of study, your work experience, and your personal pursuits, what do you know best?

Create a list of these. It will likely be a mash-up of topics both broad and specific. Like 'conceptual problem solving' and 'making ties for fly fishing.'

There's no maximum or minimum length for this list. Just strive to record any knowledge area you feel that you could teach well to an eager student.

Once you're done, this list will serve as a starting point. It helps you address the question: *What else do I need in order to acquire the right Mastery for the life I want?*

Passions, Values, and Aptitudes

Work can be joyful or it can be drudgery. What makes the difference is whether your efforts are aligned with your intrinsic motivators. *Do you enjoy the work? Is it meaningful to you? Are you good at it?*

Create another list: one focused on itemizing out your passions (what interests you), values (what guides you) and aptitudes (what you naturally excel at). Once identified, these will serve as your compass points in your quest for Mastery, helping you chart a course that plays to your innate strengths and interests.

Creating such a list can be challenging, because this is meaty, existential territory (*What guides me?* etc). But don't worry; there are a number of excellent testing services, like the Johnson O'Connor Research Foundation, designed to help surface these insights for you. Our career book contains exercises that will help as well, along with a robust list of the best testing services to consider.

Life Goals

To chart a course, you need to have a desired destination in mind. Or else you risk aimlessly wandering.

Invest time thinking hard about what you want out of life. Create as specific a vision as possible.

Think 10 years out. Where are you living? What does your home look like? What relationships are important to you? How do you spend your free time? What role do you play in your community?

Bringing your life goals into focus enables you to start understanding the necessary requirements to meet them. Let's say it's important for you to live on ten acres in a Mid-Atlantic or Southern small farming community. That gives you direction on areas to consider for relocation. Looking at real estate prices in those markets will inform how much savings and income you'll need to have to afford such a property. Planning on doing some small scale farming and ranching there? Then there's a myriad of hands-on skills you'll need to start acquiring (gardening, husbandry, permaculture, etc) if you don't already have them.

The purpose of developing such a clear, detailed picture of your life goals is to demystify the path from "where you are" to "where you want to be." The insights here answer the question: *What specific Mastery am I going to need to develop to earn and maintain this desired future?*

As with the previous steps, our career book contains discrete exercises to guide you through the visioning process.

Brutal Honesty

After completing the above steps, revisit them. Do they accurately reflect your true thoughts, feelings, beliefs and hopes?

This process of self-discovery follows the *Garbage In = Garbage Out* rule. The insights it will offer you will only be as accurate as the inputs.

If you aren't being brutally honest with yourself about your strengths and weaknesses, if you're letting your answers be swayed by what you think society thinks you should value, the results you get won't be valid. Worse, they'll send you in the wrong direction, wasting valuable time and guaranteeing your frustration.

So invest the time to review your output from the above steps, and make any revisions you deem necessary to make it as authentic as possible.

Create Your Plan

At this point, you should have a good idea of what you want to accomplish in life, which skills and resources you have to use towards those goals, and which you may be currently lacking.

The next step is to use these insights to create a roadmap for getting from where you are today to where you want to be.

Depending on your goals and current mastery, your roadmap may involve getting additional education or accreditations. Or management experience. Or demonstrating proficiency with a specific skill that's new for you. Obviously, the requirements of the plan you develop will be unique to your personal situation.

We strongly recommend working with a professional guide of some sort here, such as a career or life coach. They can offer seasoned structure to your plan development efforts, as well as suggest strategies that they know from years of experience will work.

Work Your Plan

As the old saying goes: *Plan your work, then work your plan.*

Again, the influence of a professional coach here is very valuable. They will help you remain focused, holding you to account if you're in danger of not hitting your plan's milestones. They can serve as an important sounding board as you consider making iterations to your plan based on new observations you make as you begin to implement it. And there will inevitably be setbacks, where their emotional encouragement and years of perspective will keep you convicted to persevere and achieve your goals.

To again quote Thomas Edison: *Genius is one percent inspiration, ninety-nine percent perspiration.*

The point? Once you've figured out what you need to do (inspiration), don't give up until it's done.

INTELLECTUAL KNOWLEDGE

Remember that the human brain is wired to learn in a continuous cycle. We formulate a hypothesis, test it, observe the results, and then alter our understanding through critical reflection:

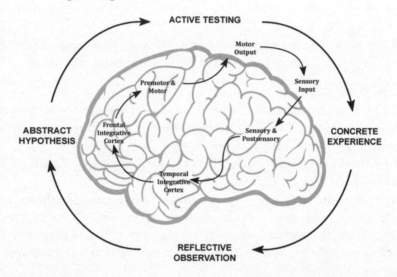

Intellectual knowledge then, is a process of re-visitation. To deepen our understanding, we need to look at a topic from different angles and perspectives—the more, the better. And after taking time to synthesize and reflect, we need to do it again. If not, we tend to forget or otherwise diminish key insights if we're not repeatedly re-visiting and challenging them.

In our own pursuit of intellectual knowledge here at Peak Prosperity, we've found the following habits very effective:

- **Pull from a large, diverse set of sources** – When seeking to learn the truth, avoid placing yourself in an 'echo chamber' where everyone parrots the same point of view. We find that an intelligent counter-argument is the best catalyst for learning, as it forces us to challenge our assumptions, clarify our rationale, and articulate the weaknesses in the opposing view.

- **Always examine the motivations of each source** – It's rare to encounter a completely unbiased source. Media outlets, think tanks, researchers, bloggers—each has a certain lens through which they perceive reality (whether they realize and/or admit it). And some have actual defined agendas. Being aware of the bias allows you to see through it, put it aside, and look for any underlying substance.

- **Seek to understand the 'Why?'** – The media primarily 'reports.' It focuses on What happened, Who was involved, and How things went down. These base facts are useful, but they don't reveal the underlying story, nor enable us to make the right decisions. If you looked out your back porch at a rich red sunset, and were pleasantly surprised to see some deer, rabbits and a fox trundle by, you might sit down to marvel at nature's beauty for a peaceful stretch. But if you instead knew that the red clouds and animal parade were caused by a massive wildfire bearing down on your house, you'd be making an entirely different set of choices. The point here is to critically assimilate all of the data you read, hear and see, and ask yourself "Why is this happening?"

- **Deepen understanding through repetition** – Those who have read Malcolm Gladwell's book *Outliers* are familiar with his assertion that roughly 10,000 hours of experience are required to become an 'expert' in a given practice, be it archery or astrophysics. Many of those hours are spent in repetitive training (drawing a bowstring or calculating spectral mass), refining one's understanding of the craft and discovering micro-learnings that incrementally improve skill. Understanding the macro story playing out around us as the Three E trends converge is no different: it requires a lot of re-visitation of the material to truly understand how our systems operate and are interconnected. How many of you reading this are rock-solid in your understanding of the debt-based nature of fiat currency, and how it is created and destroyed? Or why the lower oil prices and increased production from shale wells is a confirmation, not a contradiction, that the Peak Oil theory is accurate? This is why we built *The Crash Course* as a series of digestible video chapters: in order to allow for deeper understanding with each replaying.

EXPERIENTIAL KNOWLEDGE

Developing experiential knowledge is all about appreciating the vast difference between understanding how something works in principle and how it works in actuality. You don't "know" something until you've done it, and done it many times. Once you have, and you appreciate which different conditions produce which different outcomes, you have embodied the knowledge and started to master it.

An easy way to think of this is the apprenticeship model that began in the Middle Ages and is still used in most vocational trades. A novice works under supervision, tackling increasingly complex tasks as skill level increases over the years, until the novice is himself a master.

Developing such expertise takes time, effort and dedication. When acquiring a new skill, it's going to require a lot of repetition before you not only know how to do it well, but have encountered the unexpected edge cases and know how to handle them appropriately. It was for a good reason that apprenticeships during ancient times lasted seven years. They saw that it took that long to truly master a tradecraft.

And you can't really take shortcuts, as Chris learned when he first tried his hand at small-scale farming. Once he had his property ready for planting, he approached a local farmer who had been raising crops in the area for decades.

"How long will it take me to become a decent farmer?" Chris asked him.

"Ten years" was the reply.

"Hmmm," said Chris. "Not to boast, but I'm actually a pretty quick learner. I've got a PhD in the biosciences, and understand a lot about soil chemistry and such. For a guy like me, how long should it take?"

The farmer looked at him with new appraisal, "Oh, I see. For you then? Ten years."

"You see, you're going to have to figure out how things grow in the year with too much rain. And then in the year with too little. There's going to be the year of the strange fungus on your crops. And then the year of the little green bugs that eat everything. No matter how much study you do in advance, nature is going to surprise you. From everything I've seen in my career, it's takes at least 10 years for someone to become an experienced farmer."

So, not only does it take time to become familiar with the nuances of a new skill, but sometimes theory which makes great sense on the blackboard has unpredictable unintended consequences in the real world.

One classic example of this is the "cobra effect." During British colonial rule of India, the government became concerned about the large number of cobras in Delhi. So it issued a bounty on the poisonous snakes, paying a fixed sum for each dead cobra brought in by the public.

It didn't take long for things to start going sideways on this plan. In order to receive more payments, enterprising residents began breeding cobras.

Clearly this was not what the British rulers intended. Once they discovered how their program was being abused, they terminated the bounty scheme. And what happened next? Yep, with no incentive left, the breeders set their now-worthless snakes free. And the cobra problem in Delhi skyrocketed to much greater heights than before the bounty program began. The "solution" had the exact opposite effect as intended.

This is why you can't wait until crisis hits to acquire new skills. By then, you have no time left to put in the hours of practice, to discover all the unexpected surprise cases and their workarounds. You have to start work on them now, while the mistakes you make while climbing the learning curve have much lower consequence costs associated with them.

KEY SUCCESS FACTOR: CURIOSITY

In our many years of helping people acquire knowledge capital, there's a common success factor we've noticed. Those who demonstrate *curiosity* are much more likely to develop Mastery, both faster and in more fields than others.

And we're not the only ones to have noticed this. Albert Einstein had such a reverence for the value of inquisitiveness that he urged others to "Never lose a holy curiosity." More than that, it's what he attributed his great success to, exclaiming, "I have no special talent. I am only passionately curious."

The curious mind realizes that the more it learns, the more there is left to know. As there is no perfect state of comprehension where everything is 100% understood, it's always on the lookout for missing insights. This 'radar' enables faster notice and integration of useful information, a valuable advantage when entering an era of rapid change.

Living as we are in a time of false narratives, full of broken and manipulated signals (overly-rosy media reports, stock prices propped up by central bank intervention, etc.), it's curiosity that enables you to see the "hidden world" behind the mirage. Refusing to take at face value what you're told and shown, digging deeper into the data and critically questioning it—these are the means by which you develop a picture of the world as it truly is. And in so doing, you give yourself the power to see dangers and opportunities others cannot. Once you clearly understand the risks that are in play, you can take measures to avoid them and design solutions to exploit them—creating value for yourself and others.

So, how "passionately curious" are you? You don't have to operate at Einstein's level to reap its benefits, but you should take deliberate steps to inject more inquisitiveness into your daily approach to life.

The good news is that curiosity behaves like a muscle: it gets stronger with exercise. And similarly, research shows that critical thinking ability diminishes with neglect. It's very much a "use it or lose it" resource, so be sure to keep yours fit and strong. Read. Write down your key learnings, to articulate them to yourself and others. Debate with other curious minds. Take informed action based on your conclusions and note the results. Refine your understanding based on what you see.

In this way, you'll progress from being merely curious, to becoming *wise*.

LEVERAGING OTHERS' KNOWLEDGE

In your pursuit of knowledge, knowing what *not* to spend your time learning is as important as what is. You can't learn everything, so you need to prioritize your efforts.

Studies show again and again that playing to your strengths is far more effective than working to overcome your weaknesses.

Leveraging your natural aptitudes is much more likely to result in outperformance, often without much extra effort on your part. The work feels comfortable and often enjoyable. And the more you excel, the more rewards (pride, praise and payment) follow.

Trying to reverse a shortcoming is much harder. It requires a lot more focus, time and energy, and progress tends to be substantially more elusive. And in most cases, improvement will be modest at best and returns much lower compared to your strengths. If you're a natural introvert, no amount of social practice is going to make you a top sales executive, let alone be happy in such a position.

The real objective in developing Knowledge Capital is to build a portfolio of the areas where you have Mastery, complemented by people you will rely on who have Mastery of the important areas where you do not.

This is how lasting success in business, athletics and the sciences has always worked. By great leaders who surround themselves with partners and advisors who—together—hold all the talents and skills needed to win.

As the "great leader" of your own life, what complementary talent do you need on your team?

Review the insights reached from the Pursuing Mastery exercises above. Where are your weak spots? What kind of expertise do you need to shore them up? Who do you know who has that expertise? Create a list. Investigate and ask around to identify candidates for all of the areas you need. Reach out to ask if these folks would be willing to provide advice for you when you need it. You'll be surprised how many are flattered to be asked and willing to say *Yes*.

SEMINARS

Seminars are a particularly effective resource for advancing your knowledge base, either by introducing you to new fields of study, or by offering intensive instruction to deepen your existing expertise. And the access they provide to subject matter experts and other curious individuals is often as valuable as the learning experience itself, as beneficial relationships can often form out of the interaction.

For readers of *The Crash Course* and this book, there's at least one Peak Prosperity seminar offered each year, where we provide an experiential immersion around the most prudent actions to take today given the coming future. If that's an opportunity that interests you, you can find out when our next one will be at www.peakprosperity.com/events.

There's a wealth of other seminars and conferences that offer good learning and skill development. Here are several of the gatherings rated highly by the PeakProsperity.com audience:

- **PolyFace Farm Intensive Discovery Weekend** – provides introductory hands-on experience to basic farming and livestock practices (www.polyfacefarms.com/education/)

- **Freedom Fest** – a four-day 'free thinking' festival focusing on sound money and civil liberty (www.freedomfest.com)

- **Slow Money National Gathering** – learn about opportunities for investing capital in sustainable food networks, as well as driving positive social change (www.slowmoney.org)

PASSING THE TORCH

Finally, we believe that along with knowledge comes the responsibility to share it with others. Mentoring is another hard-wired human trait that can be immensely fulfilling for both parties. We love to share what we know and when we can do it with mastery, allowing the one being mentored to seemingly discover for themselves what we are sharing, it's an amazingly beautiful experience.

The trends that are shaping the arriving future will have massive repercussions. The more people we can make aware of them and motivate to take prudent action today, in advance, the better off we all will be.

There's an element here of "paying it forward," of enriching your community in a way that hopefully inspires others with useful knowledge to impart to follow suit.

Yet there's also a self-serving angle, too. The fewer people around you to be caught unprepared by the future translates into greater stability for your community.

So pass it on. Everybody wins.

CHAPTER 10

EMOTIONAL CAPITAL

It's pretty easy to make an argument that, of all the eight forms of capital, Emotional Capital is *the most* important one. No amount of money, possessions, and friends will matter if you lack the emotional ability to manage adversity and setback.

We all know people in our lives who remain upbeat and persevere no matter what obstacles life throws in their way. Then there are those who fall to pieces at the first whiff of difficulty. The difference between the two? Emotional resilience.

Among the people we deal with, this form of capital is typically the least developed. That's probably because most cultures encourage the suppression of feelings, and offer little if any support for emotional or spiritual literacy and depth, while reinforcing and promoting either stoicism (Clint Eastwood) or fragility (Lindsay Lohan). The stifling of emotional processing is especially prevalent among men.

Most cultures reward social obedience and conformity, which the modern education system reinforces, indoctrinating us in these traits at a young age.

So how can we go about re-programming ourselves with the kind of mental adaptability and strength that will grant us deeper Emotional Capital? How can we begin to shift towards accepting *what is* rather than fixate on what we wish to be true?

OUR REACTION DETERMINES OUR FATE

So let's start with a guarantee: *Things will not go according to your plans.* They *never* do.

You should prepare to experience surprise, disappointment and stress— likely often—as we progress through the next few turbulent decades.

When we become stressed, our bodies become flooded with stress hormones that spike our heart rates, raise our blood pressure, and shrink our ability to think clearly as our brain's amygdala triggers our "fight or flight" response. An experienced psychiatrist we know explains it this way (from the Emotional Resilience Wiki at PeakProsperity.com):

> Stressed humans also commonly experience cognitive or thinking challenges such as trouble making decisions, difficulty with remembering things, trouble concentrating, and recurring thoughts about what has happened and what we've witnessed.
>
> And our behaviors and emotions can change due to the stress we've undergone, making us more likely to be irritable or aggressive, cry more often, withdraw from our loved ones, feel terribly guilty or depressed, feel panic, engage in more risky behaviors, or "self medicate" with drugs or alcohol.
>
> We may experience a change in our relationship towards our faith, becoming angry over what has happened, losing interest in prayer, or avoiding worship settings and rituals that were formerly very important to our spiritual lives. The opposite may also happen, where there may be a renewal in faith life following a terrible loss.

Nobody knows exactly what's going to happen or when. The grand story unfolding across all three Es is highly dynamic, chaotic, and unpredictable. Whatever your preparations, there will absolutely be developments and setbacks you did not plan for.

Each unexpected twist has the chance to unsettle those with low tolerance for uncertainty and change, who lack the mental and emotional framework to be OK with change and remain fluid.

At the core of Emotional

READ:

Emotional Resilience Wiki

TOPIC:
Best Practices for Building Emotional Capital

URL and LINK:
See page 207

Resilience is this understanding: *it's not the insult that determines our fate, it's our reaction to it.* Here's one story that illustrates that perfectly.

A major economic superpower collapsed in modern times and the results were not pretty. The former USSR slowly eroded through the 1970s and 1980s under the weight of poor central planning, and then finally broke apart in 1989. When Ernest Hemingway was asked how he went broke he replied, *"Slowly, then all at once."* It seems that people and nations have that in common.

With startling speed, the USSR economic model collapsed and the union shattered back into Russia and a host of satellite states. The economy of Russia tumbled and crumbled. Millions of jobs were lost and desperation set in. Things were perhaps not as individually grim for Russians as would have been true for their Western counterparts because in Russia at least everybody lived in government housing and had access to government supplied food. As shabby and tasteless as these provisions might have been, their presence at least meant that nobody was starving under a bridge. Well, a few probably were, but it was not because they lived in a system that enforced that outcome.

Despite the basic support of food and housing, a shocking statistic emerged: in the eight years after the collapse of the USSR, alcohol was responsible for or involved in 54% of all deaths recorded in Russia. More than half! A normal statistic for a healthy country is around 4%.

What happened in Russia? Well, they do have a hard drinking culture there, to be sure, so that was a factor (see the upcoming chapter on Cultural Capital). But there was more to it than that. The surge in the extraordinary number of alcohol related deaths is explained by the fact that people gave up, sought to numb themselves by drinking, and these behaviors sprang from the stories that these people told themselves.

Here's what we mean. When the Russian economy collapsed and people lost their jobs, many people (but especially middle-aged men) also lost their sense of *who they were* because that was tied to their careers.

So when Dmitri the pipefitter lost his job, he thought to himself *"I am worthless now. I cannot provide for my family, my wife thinks less of me, and my friends do, too. All of this is quite shameful and painful, so I think I'll go have a few drinks."*

And a few became many, and many became too many, and eventually Dmitri lost more than his job.

It turns out that alcohol is the #1 drug humans have discovered for masking shame. There's nothing better yet in our pharmacy. The more shame you carry, the more likely it is that drinking will appeal to you.

But imagine if our pipefitter Dmitri had a different narrative running through his head when he lost his job? What if his inner narrative instead went something like this? *"This is great news! I have always wanted to have free time to explore new ideas and learn new skills and now I can do that. The collapse of our economy is sure to also have an equal measure of new opportunities to match the destruction, I just have to remain alert and figure out what they are. I am so excited by what is now happening!"*

His future would have undoubtedly turned out very differently.

In truth, the period right after the fall of the old USSR was one of the most accelerated periods of wealth transfer and economic opportunity in modern history. Many Russians became fabulously rich, as in *oligarch rich*, as a consequence of seeing the new opportunities and seizing them. Perhaps not fairly, and perhaps not in ways that everyone would see as praiseworthy, but personal opportunity was there for the taking. Some people prospered and some failed.

What separated the victors from the losers in that scramble was literally nothing more, and nothing less, than *the stories they had running through their minds.*

If you see yourself as a victim of circumstances—then *congratulations!*—you indeed are a victim of circumstances.

Or if you believe that every moment has opportunities and that your job is to figure out what those are then, *congratulations!* Fortune is smiling upon you.

Henry Ford, the automobile magnate, stated this same concept quite pithily when he said, "Whether you think you can, or you think you can't—you're right."

That's the lesson here: watch the stories you have running, know that they are never "the truth" (although they always feel like they are), and that it is within your power to reject a bad narrative and adopt a different one.

The other lesson from our Russian drinking story is this: it's not going to be the economic collapse that kills most people, but their reaction to it.

YOU ARE THE ONLY THING YOU CAN FULLY CONTROL

Again, you can't control what happens to you in life, but you *can* control how you react to it. Indeed, your reactions are the only thing you can control with 100% certainty.

What drives our responses are the stories we run in our heads, our personal narratives about ourselves and how the world works. If our identity is wrapped around the narrative *I'm wealthy*, then what happens if that money goes away? Have we have lost all of our personal value? It will seem that way if we let something as narrow as money define us. Or our job. Or our role as a parent.

In short, it is our thoughts that shape our experiences, not the other way around.

"Nothing ever is good or bad, but thinking makes it so."
                                        —Shakespeare in *MacBeth*

If the economy suddenly freezes and you lose your job, how will you react? If you're a Hollywood animator or a corporate lawyer and the world suddenly needs a lot fewer of those folks, how easily can you pivot and begin a new phase of life?

What will you do if your stored food turns out to be rotten when you open it during an emergency? If you have to pull together with your neighbors during troubled times, with tempers and emotions running high, will you be among those shouting or withdrawing, or will you be a calming influence around which people can rally?

How about today? Can you honestly say that you're living with joy, purpose and a deep sense of fulfillment? Or do you have some remaining inner work to do? (That was a trick question; everyone has more work to do.)

Most assume that we know ourselves pretty well, better than anyone else, at least. But those who commit to active introspection are almost universally surprised to discover how blind they were to their own inner shadows. In fact, we've yet to meet *anyone* who has completed that process of self-discovery, probably because the Buddha or his equivalent has never dropped by for a visit.

As we begin to dig, we uncover our shadows, those parts of ourselves that lurk deep within and, unseen, drive our behaviors and actions.

"Until you make the unconscious conscious, it will direct your life and you will call it fate."

                                        —Carl Jung

What we think of as "me" or "I"—our conscious self—is not actually a fixed entity, immovable and rigid. Instead, each of us is a collection of emotional experiences, many from our earliest and wordless days as infants, that are jumbled together into this identity we call "me."

What triggers joy or rage, happiness or depression, in each of us is unique. While our emotional responses may feel completely justified, as if our response were some sort of a universal truth, they usually aren't.

What angers you may delight someone else, and have no impact at all on a third person.

The key to better self-control comes from better self-understanding of these idiosyncrasies that make each of us unique. That understanding can be achieved through active introspection, therapy, meditation, and other similar pursuits. Once we identify the triggers that drive our reactions, we can set to work on re-wiring them in ways that serve us better.

Here's a story from one of our readers that shows how one can find a higher degree of self-awareness and happiness by focusing inwards:

> I loved the idea of building a homestead and thriving in a sustainable way. And I started out doing everything I could do to become more resilient. But I soon found that I also needed to change. I wasn't happy with my world, with my government, but also I wasn't really happy with myself.
>
> I had some idea of what I might do from practicing yoga in my youth but had no idea of the path or what the outcome might be. I just wanted to feel better and be happier and that was it.
>
> So I started practicing yoga and meditation without any particular religion in mind. I felt better, but found I wanted to do this in a community so I started going to classes, which lead to teacher trainings, retreats, new friends, new skills, improved self-confidence and a new relationship with the universe.
>
> I could say that I became more spiritual and happy but that wouldn't really be the point. The point is that I became more in tune with living a sustainable and happy life through personal growth and community engagement. And I would say that if you want to change your world you have to really think about changing yourself and your relationship with everything. Here are a few observations that I can make about my personal journey so far.
>
> 1. I don't feel like anyone or anything is doing anything to me anymore. I am responsible for my destiny.
>
> 2. I don't really have too many negative, worrisome thoughts or stress. Instead my mind is mostly neutral on various subjects and I try to let my intuition determine my actions, not my emotions.
>
> 3. My diet changed to primarily vegetarian, I stopped drinking. I lost weight and several physical symptoms of stress and age including acid-reflux and eczema.

4. Even though my wife and family don't practice what I do, the entire family dynamic changed and is much more loving and supportive.

5. I found new friends, new skills, and new communities intent on friendship, support, and change (personal and the world).

6. Work and life seem to be much less work and more of a joy

I realize that yoga and meditation may seem a little hippie-ish or religious to many folks. Hey, I am an executive in Silicon Valley so it was a stretch for me too. I just wanted to share this here because I think it's a big part of resiliency for the future and I hope you do to.

The key message that this reader summarizes so well is that our happiness is found inside of us. It's not out there in the physical world, waiting for us to come get it like some conquistador. Instead, it resides within our ability to improve ourselves where we can, accept ourselves where we can't, and appreciate the combination of both—which defines who we are. From this flows happiness, love, compassion, and contentment—things all independent of how much or how little "stuff" you own.

NARRATIVE SHIFTING

There are a thousand paths to inner enlightenment and it's not for us to tell you which will work best for you. However, we *can* tell you what has worked well for many of the folks we work with through Peak Prosperity's website and seminars.

"Narrative shifting" is an extremely powerful tool to have at your disposal and it works like this. Suppose two people are walking down the street and happen to pass by someone walking in the other direction, who happens to laugh at the exact moment their paths cross.

The first of the two people is insecure. He assumes that he's the one being laughed at. His brain starts stewing on the insult and he becomes flushed with anger, possibly shame, and maybe sadness. He walks on, consumed with fate's cruelty in making him the target of a complete stranger's mockery.

He might ruminate on this for days, and possibly internalize the experience as reinforcement of a life belief that *"People just don't like me."* All from a passing chuckle.

The other person in this story, however, has a different inner narrative running, one with a lot more positivity. When she hears the laugh, she's thrilled and grateful to have been witness to someone sharing their joy.

What luck! To be near that person right as they laughed! Her spirits are lifted, she feels like she's received a gift. *Life is good*, she thinks, as she continues on with a newfound spring in her step.

What happened here was that two people had an identical experience, but entirely different reactions to it. It was their inner narratives that determined how each perceived the event. This little story is effective in illustrating that when it comes to the narratives we tell ourselves, perception is indeed reality.

Think of these narratives as inner tape players, ready to play when pressed by some external stimulus. While it seems like one response was "better" than the other, and we would certainly choose the happier one, the practice of Zen would seek to have neither reaction, but to simply observe the laughing person without assigning it any emotional impact. Simply: "*Ah, a person is laughing.*"

Whether that Zen-like state of grace is a destination you seek or not, there's a lot we can benefit from by shifting, shaping and controlling our inner narratives to our advantage.

Step one is simply being aware that you have these tapes running in your head. When you find yourself becoming emotionally triggered, do your best to ask yourself: "*What are my narratives telling me?*"

Capturing this is pure gold. Because once you know the main narratives in play, you can start deconstructing them: How did they form? What influenced their development? Do they seem accurate? Are they serving you well, or creating unnecessary conflict?

Step two, which is trickier, is to work at consciously inserting a replacement narrative for any you feel aren't working well. If you were the slighted party in our example above, you might just try out a few different 'explanations' to see how they feel: "*What if that person was laughing at my partner, not me.*" Or you might try "*I'll bet that person was just remembering a bit from a comedy show they saw last night.*" Or maybe "*What if they had an ear bud in the other ear that I couldn't see, and a friend was telling them a joke over the phone?*"

As you begin to practice narrative shifting, you'll notice that your emotional reactions shift, in response. What this practice does is begins to loosen the grip our unconscious has on what we see and how we interpret it. Without a fixed set of pre-recorded reactions, we're free to adapt and improvise, and by doing so, very much determine the reality we experience. We become more in control of our destiny.

This makes "narrative shifting" one of the most important tools of emotional resilience.

And it also helps us cope with the large issues outside of our individual influence, too.   Here's another example. Imagine that you're utterly distraught at the impact humans are having on the natural world. The planetary ravages of pollution, greenhouse gases, and resource exploitation fill you with grief. On one level, humans' desecration of the Earth is very real and can't be disputed.

But what if we take three giant steps backwards? What if we shift the narrative from our own personal lifetime to one that spans millions of years? With this as our frame of reference, there's literally nothing humans can really do to permanently harm the Earth. It has already shucked off 99.9% of all species that ever lived, and undergone mass extinctions that make today's look like a child's tea party. It has always recovered. No matter how much damage humans do in their time on Earth, the planet will bounce back and cover itself with life anew, just possibly without humans aboard.

By shifting the narrative, we can see that the Earth will be quite fine with or without us and therefore there's nothing to grieve.

This larger narrative accomplishes two things. It helps to lessen our grief for something we have no individual control over, and focuses our efforts away from "saving the Earth" (it's fine, it doesn't need saving) and towards something we possibly can impact: *saving ourselves.*

THE GREAT CHALLENGE

What all of this focuses back towards is that the coming times are going to demand the most from us, and that's a good thing. It's far too easy to sit back in comfort and let life slip by as if it were a dress rehearsal instead of the real thing. If you're like us, though, it feels shallow and unsatisfying to live the life society is asking of us. To focus on consuming, to be a good worker drone—aren't your unique gifts aching to come out in a more real and authentic way?

To let them flourish, you have to challenge your inner narratives, what your culture expects of you, what the media is (mis)directing you to focus on, and your own self-imposed limitations.

As another Peak Prosperity reader shares, it's about asking the big questions:

> I was hungry for the big picture. *The Crash Course* rounded up much of the data I was struggling to take in and offered such a useful perspective that I've been mesmerized by the website and community for years. But my forte is not data. I have no post-secondary training in stats or logic or economics. My talent is

in navigating the inward territory, where the data impacts our assumptions, beliefs, attachments, misconceptions, emotions and unique human strengths.

Every painful new understanding of how civilization is behaving requires journeys into the inner world. What part of my unconsciously held worldview is now being challenged? What feelings come with that?

More outraged naivety? Confusion? Fear? Grief? And always, under the stack, love, huge love for this planet and her biosphere. Then comes the mental work. What perception is closer to truth than the one that is dissolving? Something that doesn't exist yet? What might it be and how can I bring it to life? I enjoy this intricate work, a kind of mending that requires heart, brain, spirit, body, community, and connection with our planet. Even the grief and fear can be experienced with purpose: the reclamation of human minds from a terribly untrue narrative, and the development of a biosphere-compliant human civilization. Not boring!

I find Chris and Adam's call for the development of a new narrative compelling and important. What is the purpose and potential of a human lifespan on Earth in these times? How does a human being, inherently full of intelligence, gratitude and love, remain its lively self in the midst of such massive foolishness? What story of life on Earth could include us all, all humans, all of the biosphere, and let us move to a way of life with a beautiful future? There is a tiny question at the bottom of this stack. Just how far can we go if we insist on being our true, unrepressed, brilliant, problem-solving selves, full of deep love for our planet home, even here at the chaotic, gritty, dangerous end of empire, of civilization and of biosphere as we know them?

These questions get right down to the heart of it all: "*What, really, is the point of life?*" People have been asking this question since the beginning of humans, and we have always sought meaning and our place in the universe.

The best part about the turbulent period ahead of us is that the clear need for making changes gives us the opportunity for re-invention. As a society, as communities and as individuals. You have the opportunity to make radical shifts in how you live your life—it all depends on your courage and willingness to define what you want, and to pursue it with perseverance. You just need to be willing to walk away from what's comfortable (if it's indeed not serving you) and embrace the challenge of re-imagining life as you think it should be.

MASTERING STRESS

More mentally resilient people share a number of common traits. At the top of this list is having a support system of friends and family who can share in the struggles.

Humans are a social species; we need each other. To enrich our lives. To lean on for help when we need it. Without the support of others—both physical and emotional—we're capable of much less.

Understanding how your body functions under stress will help you recognize when it threatens to derail you. In an agitated state, it's much harder for others to help you, and for you to be open to receiving their efforts, let alone make good decisions.

When these moments arise, there are coping mechanisms you can use to defuse the anxiety. Here are the ones the Navy Seals use (and those guys deal with a LOT of stress!):

1. **Goal setting.** The ability to reason and plan helps to keep the stress and chaos at bay. No matter how bad the situation, always have a goal even if that goal is simply *one more breath*.

2. **Mental rehearsal and visualization.** This aligns the body and mind so that stressful gaps between the two don't arise or are minimized. Mentally rehearsing scenarios allows things to unfold more effortlessly and naturally when they actually arise. So you might pre-rehearse what it would be like if you lost your job.

3. **Self-talk.** Self-talk, especially positive self-talk, has a powerful calming influence on the mind and body. *Okay, self, we're going to make it through this and have a great story for the campfire later...*

4. **Arousal control.** Slow, deep breathing delivers more oxygen to the brain and tells the body that everything is okay. After all, we're breathing long and slow aren't we? This practice can enhance brain awareness and alertness.

The reason that the Navy has a program to control the mind-body reactions is because they know that the emotional core of the brain (that pesky amygdala again!) is what takes over when things get dicey. It's nothing to be ashamed of, it's simply how we're wired neurologically. But often our culture demands that we act as if it doesn't exist.

Which is why, even if we're not in a panic-inducing crisis, the same low-grade anxiety-producing responses can be churning along, reducing our motivation, slowly inflaming our body and ruining our daily joy and long-term health.

To combat the low-level aspect of this fear response, we recommend the following:

- **Meditation** has been proven to be one of the very best tools for centering our minds and calming ourselves. Which of the staggering number of options for meditation is right for you—tai chi, yoga, Zen, mindfulness, guided thought, or just quiet reflection in a warm bath—is yours to decide.

- **Physical activity**. Beyond those mentioned in the chapter on Living Capital, the benefits of physical activity on healthy brain functioning has been proven and re-proven so many times that the matter is settled. It's very important.

- **Sleep**. Get lots of good sleep, as much as your body says it needs. In our modern world, of nightly smart phones in bed, working on computers until late, and television watching are common things. Unfortunately the blue light emitted from these devices interferes with our sleep patterns by interrupting our melatonin production. Functional medicine expert Dr. Chris Kresser recommends wearing amber colored glasses two hours before bed time if you are watching screens. The amber color filters out the blue light and Dr. Kresser says that more often than not people with long-standing sleep issues report them being entirely cured in just a few days.

- **Play**. Play has physical, emotional and cognitive benefits. We use it to form new neural pathways and practice reacting to the unexpected. As humans, we are literally wired for it, but our culture does a good job of shaming us away from it after childhood. Do your body and mind a favor—make time for play.

- **Make new and/or deeper social connections.** Our social networks are essential to our mental and emotional well-being. Chris has belonged to a men's group for the past 10 years. It is enormously important to him as a source of social nourishment and emotional strength. The group engages in everything from tasks like cider making to events like hunting trips, in addition to their regular emotional check-in sessions where anything and everything is opened up for discussion and processing.

As with the other preparations mentioned in this book, those who develop some degree of mastery with these today will be tremendously better off than those who wait. Indeed, it may be extremely difficult to start from scratch with these once a crisis strikes.

THE SPIRITUAL SIDE

For the majority of people, a big part of emotional resilience is rooted in spiritual connection.

This is tricky territory so we'll begin by saying that it's not our intent here to elevate or malign any one religion over another. But we do wholeheartedly support the idea of developing spiritual purpose in whatever way is meaningful for you. Some find it in organized faith. Some find it in nature. Some find it in science. Some find it inside themselves.

We are all tested in life, by trials and tribulations and, ultimately, by confronting our mortality. If your emotional resilience is what helps you react well during these tests, it's your spiritual resilience that gives you the conviction to push through them.

Keeping the perspective that we are part of a bigger story arc allows us to understand that the world is not set against us personally, and that there are larger processes in play for the universe, the planet, humanity and our communities. Each of us has a role to play in each of these gigantic processes, no matter how small. Realizing this puts our personal egos and challenges into perspective. From this sense of humility, peace, compassion and love result.

There's a great mystery to life and seeking meaning is a noble pursuit that has always been a part of being human. There are a great many spiritual teachers out there and if you have an open mind, there's something to be gained from listening to a range of them. Borrow the insights from each that resonate for you.

By combining a spiritual worldview with the self-mastery exercises in this chapter you should be able to handle well nearly any kind of adversity you encounter.

Remember, it's not the insult that determines your fate. It's your reaction to it.

The good news? That's something you're 100% in control of.

CHAPTER 11

SOCIAL CAPITAL

As social creatures, with all of our gifts and flaws, strengths and weaknesses, the simple truth is: we *need* each other.

We rely on people in our community to do the things for us that we can't do well ourselves, but the biggest need is for the emotional nourishment that we receive from each other.

It's more than telling that one of the most punitive forms of punishment that humans have ever devised is prolonged solitary confinement. With enough time in isolation, some people are irretrievably damaged. What's also interesting is that we've never been so technologically connected, yet so physically and emotionally isolated from each other. It's as if we've self-imposed solitary confinement on ourselves to the point that we could be in a crowded room yet feel all alone.

Our physical and emotional, intimate connections with each other nourish us in ways that are difficult to measure, but easy to detect. Touch and eye contact are wired into us as necessary elements of healthy living.

Deep interpersonal connections are what bring fulfillment and meaning to our lives. We all crave to be given the opportunity to bring our gifts into the world, and the reflections of caring people who really know us are essential to that process.

We want to be really seen, to mentor, to give and receive, to express our unique gifts, and to express those gifts in each of the roles we can fill as we age from infants to elders. At least that's how it's supposed to work.

Seamless and joyous transitions through life's developmental stages happen best when we are part of a whole and intact community. While such communities are rare, and some readers may doubt they even exist, they are increasingly being sought out and created by people, especially younger people who have decided that there's more to life than an isolated consumer-driven lifestyle. They are seeking the more connected and authentic relationships for which we are all innately wired.

One of the very best realizations that can emerge from a wider perspective on the predicaments we face is that life is not to be wasted, that present-day circumstances are demanding that we bring our very best selves forward, and that our relationships are as essential to our own happiness as they are to the fate of the world.

Taken together, all of our relationships and experiences with the people around us form, over time, what is called Social Capital. With Social Capital, we can call in favors, anticipate needs, reach out to give and receive support, witness and participate in important life events, and weave the strands that become ropes of connection over time.

Most people intuitively understand the importance of Social Capital, but strangely, in our experience, it's quite often an under-invested area. Many people seriously underestimate the time and dedicated effort that is required to build true community. It's not something you can purchase and be "done" with, the way you can with food storage preparations or a solar installation. And it's not something you can immediately create for yourself no matter how socially gifted you might be.

Here's a situation we've run into before. One person in a relationship will peer into the future, run a few mental calculations, and suddenly proclaim: *"Honey, we need to move to the country!"*

This person might think that they need to move really far out into the country, away from people, even the ones they already know, in order to be safe. This might make some tactical sense, at least under certain scenarios, but at a cost their partner is unwilling to bear.

What these people who seek safety at a distance are missing out on is the concept that *social connections* are as valuable as any other asset they might own. They are critically important not just to our happiness but also our potential future security. That is, one's Social Capital really matters. On this front, moving away sometimes makes sense; other times it really does not.

We each value different things in different ways. For the person who has always measured worth in dollars or personal accomplishments, the actual value of Social Capital can be an unfamiliar concept. Similarly, the person who wishes to protect his or her family by moving farther away may be undervaluing the strength and importance of the connections that their partner or children have already forged right where they live.

Social Capital is a very real and highly valuable commodity; one that takes time to build no matter how motivated or gifted one may be at forming connections.

FORGET ABOUT GOING IT ALONE OR MOVING AT THE LAST MINUTE

As discussed earlier, the "lone wolf" archetype is largely a myth when it comes to facing the challenges of life. None of us can go it alone and be fully resilient. And who wants to live an isolated existence, anyways?

As the descent into a lower net-energy lifestyle places increasing limits on our way of life, and as volatility further builds in our economy and environmental systems, we're going to be increasingly dependent on others to obtain much of what we take for granted today.

During the coming periods of upheaval and hardship—whether it takes the form of a natural disaster (Katrina), an outage of key resources (gas lines during the 1970s), or a sovereign default (Greece 2015)—it's going to be those of us with networks of resourceful, willing, and trusted neighbors that fare best.

Given the direction things are going in, our connections to each other will become even more important in the future. Plan all you want and store up as much material capital as you can, but eventually circumstances will outpace your planning and outlast your stuff. What will you do then? How will you cope? The answer is that you will succeed in direct proportion to the depth and durability of your social connections.

Recent history shows this is indeed the case, as we learned from our podcasts with various experts who have chronicled the collapses within Zimbabwe and Argentina.

We're constantly amazed at the number of people who have the attitude that they'll get serious about developing community once the storm clouds of crisis become visible. Perhaps they'll make an emergency dash to an existing community they know about or to an acquaintance's property somewhere. You know, once things get serious enough.

By then, of course, it will be much too late to expect an easy transition to that new life, because that will

> **LISTEN:**
>
>
>
> *Fernando Aguirre Podcast*
>
> **TOPIC:**
> *Surviving Argentina's Hyperinflation*
>
> **URL and LINK:**
> *See page 207*

depend on having robust and functional relationships based on trust and sharing already in place.

Others take an overly hopeful view that, should times get tough, they'll just relocate to another country and insert themselves there. While, yes, that's a possibility, it's unrealistic to expect the local residents to warmly and openly embrace an unknown outsider who suddenly shows up right before or during a crisis. It's much more probable that newcomers will be treated with wariness or hostility by the locals until such time as they have built authentic social connections with the community.

This is one of the reasons that we regularly council people to think long and hard before deciding to move to another country. Unless you are both moving there and marrying into a big, well-loved local family, you run the risk of being shunned or even targeted if/when times get tough.

THE FOUNDATIONS OF COMMUNITY

At first our interactions with people are going to be transactional in nature before they become relational. You will do something for them and they will reciprocate. Over time these experiences will thicken, like ropes spun one thread at a time, into something lasting and based on trust.

It's unfortunate, but true, that when under stress, humans think from a baser, more survival-oriented cognitive level. The fight-or-flight mechanism becomes triggered and responses tend to revert to simplified "friend" or "foe" decisions. You want to be seen as friend not foe whenever possible.

How do you accomplish this? By creating a shared history of favorable interactions over time, well in advance of any rough spots. Actions speak louder than words, which means that when the chips are down it will be your past actions that help people answer these questions about you: *Will this person be there for me? Can I trust them? Am I better off with them around?* Nothing will come any where near as close as your past actions and behavior in influencing hearts and minds.

How do you go about creating these favorable interactions? There are four excellent ways to begin weaving your social ropes:

- Involving Yourself
- Creating Reasons for Engagement
- Being in Service
- Giving *and* Receiving

Involve Yourself

Become an active participant in the existing structure of the community around you. From church groups, to neighborhood watches, to volunteer committees, to sports clubs, to local government—every city and town has a myriad of social organizations to 'plug into'. Some are formal in structure, like the Rotary Club; others are completely homespun, as with a book club or discussion group or playing music.

The first critical step to building community is to *get involved*. Discover what the options are for participation in your area and pick at least one to involve yourself in.

Yes, you're busy. And yes, there are more demands on your time than you have hours in the day. But unless you prioritize these social interactions and consciously carve out time for them they won't happen. So, commit to the investment and protect that commitment.

Not sure how to get started?

Your local community center will have a robust list of prospects. Skimming the community calendar of your local paper (or its website) will highlight events over the coming week you can drop in on. Call the churches and schools in your area—they always have projects and productions for which you can be an audience member or volunteer. Join a gym or a local club for your favorite sport. Or try your hand at community service.

Or, try this: The next time you're asked to be part of something—chaperoning a field trip for your child's school, volunteering at the local food bank, taking a dance class, feeding the neighbors' cat while they're away, *whatever* it is—just say "yes." This is the low-effort way to get your social feet wet. And you'll soon find that once you make yourself available to others, your appreciated contributions will soon lead to more invitations to engage in other opportunities.

Creating Reasons for Engagement

Once you plug into some of the activities already underway in your area, you become, by definition, a member of the community. You're now an active part of it. And certain recognitions and benefits come along with that—you're no longer an outsider, and people begin to genuinely care for you the more they interact with and get to know you.

All this is good, very good, actually. But it gets even better if you step up as a leader. While this could mean throwing your hat in the ring to be President of the local Lions Club or joining the PTA Board, it doesn't have to be anything nearly that formal, structured or commitment-heavy.

It simply means taking initiative to create new opportunities for people to work together for their mutual well-being.

It could be hosting a single neighborhood potluck get-together at your house. Or starting a petition for a local cause you believe in. Or finding a few fellow musicians to join you in the park once a week for a jam session. Just look around your community and ask: *What's missing? What could make things better?* And then think on what role, given your abilities and interests, you can play in filing those gaps.

The more people who view you as an agent for the common good, the greater your Social Capital. Think of this as a 'social insurance policy' you pay for with acts of goodwill versus money.

Being in Service

Along this same line, the most effective and direct path to building and strengthening ties with others is to provide welcome support during times of need.

Modern society has done much to isolate us from one another and keep our social interactions at the superficial "everything is fine" level. The virtual world of technology, suburban fences and urban walls, the social shaming of failure—all conspire to make it a challenge to admit to our neighbors when we're troubled, let alone ask them for help. Which is why the neighbor who asks, unprompted *What can I do for you?* is so greatly appreciated.

And life gives us plenty of openings to ask that question, and to 'be in service' in ways that truly matter to the recipients. The young couple who just had a baby? Bringing over a home-cooked meal or offering to handle a few of their household chores will earn you a massive amount of gratitude. The woman whose husband just died unexpectedly? She could very well use some help with the funeral planning, or just need someone to talk with to ease the sorrow and loneliness. The elderly man around the corner? Shoveling his front steps after a snowfall only takes a few minutes, but could save him from a broken hip. The possibilities to be a helping hand are endless.

READ:

📖

How to Build Community

TOPIC:
Best Practices for Building Social Capital

URL and LINK:
See page 207

These are the opportunities in which true social capital is earned, and because you're choosing to 'do the right thing,' it feels good while earning it. Being in service in this way is something every one of us can do, regardless of our physical or financial condition. You'll note that most of the examples above require no money to be spent, nor any physical prowess.

The message here is to open your eyes. To what's going on in the lives of those around you, and to the entry points life is offering you to step in and make a positive difference. The more times you do, the more your odds increase that others will reciprocate when you find yourself in need.

Giving and Receiving

Giving and receiving form an energetic loop. Being in service is, surprisingly, far easier for most people than being on the receiving end of the equation. Asking for and receiving help is a very uncomfortable gesture, much more socially difficult than giving. Some of the negative attachments people place on receiving are that it is a sign of weakness that places you in debt to another.

There are nearly unlimited opportunities to give to others in the form of time, food, money, labor or other resources. It's not hard to find ways to give. However, if all you do is give, as generous as that may feel to you, it leaves a lot of potential Social Capital on the table, unused.

The challenge for many is to learn to receive gracefully and without hesitation: to say "yes" promptly and with gratitude so that the giver feels welcomed and appreciated for their efforts. This closes the loop and allows the giving and receiving energy to flow.

If there's nobody willing to receive, then there's no opportunity to give. In an environment like this, this potent form of Social Capital building will not be a part of your community. The challenge then is to find ways to activate both the giving and the receiving sides of the exchange so that more and more opportunities and moments of giving and receiving happen.

As you build up the skill of receiving—and it is a gracious art form—be gentle with yourself if your early attempts are as rusty and awkward as ours were. Just like anything, it takes time to become good at it.

CREATING RELATIONSHIPS WITH MEANING

As you interact socially using the methods just described, it's helpful to be aware of the degrees by which you can 'know' others.

By understanding better those you're in partnership with, and helping them understand you more intimately in return, you become aware of how best to support each other, and what you can—and can't—depend on each other for.

The following pyramid visual illustrates the major 'degrees of knowing people.' The top layer is the most superficial, and the bottom the most substantial:

Most non-family relationships in modern society remain at the highest level: We simply know **what people do**. Your co-workers, your neighbor the butcher, and the kids on the next street over who play whiffle ball in the front yard on weekend nights.

You may have a "smile-hello" relationship with these folks, know their names, and may engage in friendly chit-chat now and then, but you likely don't know much more about them than what you've directly observed them doing.

Your knowledge of people at this level has value. You can begin to start assessing whether or not you'd like to learn more about them and go deeper into a relationship, and figuring out what sorts of talents, attributes, skills, or resources they might have. Knowing what someone does professionally, or noticing evidence of a passion (a boat trailer in the driveway, for instance), are good initial indicators of useful mastery they may possess.

The foundation for friendship is laid when you take enough time to develop an understanding of **who people are**. At this next level, you'll learn a person's backstory; details like where they grew up and went to school, whether they enjoy their job, what they like to do after work, and with whom they like to spend their free time. This context helps you answer questions like: *Is this person a good fit for me? Are they someone I want to be* *closer with?* This information will help you begin to decide what kind of a relationship you'd like to foster with this person.

Next comes learning **how people react**, where you'll build on your understanding of their backstory and develop confidence in being able to predict what they'll do and say in a wide variety of circumstances. This knowledge comes from observation over time, so the number of people you'll understand in this way, out of necessity, will be substantially fewer than those relationships at the two prior levels. Watching how people behave in good times and bad (especially 'bad,' as people tend to have their core structures revealed by stress) will answer important questions like: *Does this person make good decisions? Can they keep a cool head under pressure? Do they treat me the way I want to be treated? Are they trustworthy? Dependable?* With these insights, you'll now have a much better ability to determine who's a good candidate for your inner circle and who isn't.

Lastly, once you dig deep enough to learn **why people react the way they do**, the context that frames their decision-making, you've developed a true understanding of who they are. You will know *why* they do what they do—the past wounds and experiences that have shaped their character, their values, and their beliefs. At this level you can clearly see the motivators that drive their behavior (some of which they, themselves, might be unaware of) and even predict how they will react to new situations. This gives you the confidence of knowing whom you can depend on for certain things, and under which circumstances. Further, you'll know how you can best support them as they navigate and grow through life's tougher moments.

The way to progress down this pyramid is to engage in increasingly meaningful interactions with the people around you. When you're with someone worthy of the investment, whatever level of 'knowing' you're currently at with them, actively push yourself to seek out ways to either explore this level further or attempt to deepen things and reach the next one.

One of the best ways to do this, paradoxically, is by being vulnerable. Be true and authentic and reveal who you *really* are, and you will lead the way, allowing those around you to reveal more of who they are.

HAVING EXPERIENCES THAT AREN'T ABOUT MONEY

In your efforts to create meaningful experiences with other people, be very cautious when money is involved. Typically, when money is exchanged, the dynamic changes, turning an interaction into a *transaction*.

A transaction is short-lived and final. And for the most part, impersonal. Once money moves from person A to person B, the encounter is, for all practical purposes, over. Neither party feels an increased sense of investment in the other, nor experiences a sense of favor from the exchange. In short, social capital is rarely created by trading financial capital for goods and services.

But, when you take money out of the picture, it opens a door through which each party can bring whichever of their own personal gifts (time, skills, talents, etc.) best suits the interaction. This shifts the dynamic from a sterile commercial exchange into something more. Effort is involved and a doorway is opened that will not close as quickly as when just cash is involved.

While a non-monetary experience can be a specific exchange (your neighbor agrees to let you borrow his pressure washer if you mow his lawn), there's a much wider spectrum of possible options that can lead to these more open-ended interactions. Inviting the neighborhood over for a pot-luck dinner, and playing music around a group campfire, or watching a friend's children while she runs errands are a few examples

Social economist Charles Eisenstein sagely notes that much of what used to be funded by Social Capital in previous generations are now things that we pay for. This trend has not only made us poorer financially, as we're spending money on things that used to be 'free,' but we suffer from decreased social interactions as well.

Entertainment is a good example. People used to gather to make music and song together, at church or in home parlors or back porches. Now instead, we pay over $300 per ticket, on average, to watch rock stars perform on a coliseum stage, or we watch Netflix in our bedrooms, out of sight and disconnected from interaction with real people.

Sports is much the same. In eras past, weekends were a time when families played together at the local ballpark, or paid a dollar or two to watch the local high school or bush league teams plays. Today, families instead flock to Major League Baseball stadiums where it costs several hundred dollars for a family of four to attend an average game—and that's not assuming any pre-game tailgating costs.

Similarly, childcare has become a substantial financial expense for many young families. Prior to the rise of the two-income household, neighbors would share the work of watching each other's children during the day. Parents had windows of time where they could handle whatever errands needed doing, while their children were socialized in a safe environment amongst people familiar to them. Contrast this to today, when a huge number of working families—most without nearby family or community support to lean on—pay on average $972 a month for daycare. That's a lot of money, more than many of these families can spend without making major sacrifices elsewhere in their financial budgets. And more important, the children are being raised apart from their parents and community for the majority of the day.

These are all examples of how replacing social capital with financial capital usually results in a trade-off that makes us worse off. Eisenstein heeds us to start thinking in reverse: *How I can replace financial capital with social capital?* Think on what activities in your life you can start funding with your energies and talents instead of your pocketbook.

Try it. You'll see how removing money from the equation ultimately makes you richer on more dimensions than just the dollars you save.

BEING YOUR BEST SELF

One of the most valuable benefits of building community is that it gives us a near-unlimited amount of opportunities to step into and develop our better selves.

Each interaction is a chance to be the person you've always aspired to. Are you kind? Funny? Generous? Wise? Your repeated social involvement with those around you is a gift, one that grants you a continuous stream of attempts to work on being exactly who you want to be.

This is a gift to grab with both hands, for several reasons, but most important, in building social capital, authenticity is key. People can tell when you're falsely hiding your true motives—say, asking for a favor you have no intent on returning. Sooner or later, they determine the truth. And nothing destroys social capital faster than betrayal of trust. As the saying goes:

> *Trust takes years to build,*
> *Seconds to lose,*
> *And forever to repair.*

So, whenever possible, strive to be your authentic self. You'll feel best. And others will know you accurately, and learn how best to connect with you.

Who *wouldn't* want to live this way?

CHAPTER 12

CULTURAL CAPITAL

"**C**ulture" defines the space we live in. It's the collective aspects of life shared by the people around you. What personality is to an individual, culture is to a society.

It determines much about how those in a certain group will behave and think. Its influence begins at an early age as we observe and listen to those around us, and is reinforced by our social experiences and by what the media encourages us to pay attention to.

Culture is often compared to an iceberg:

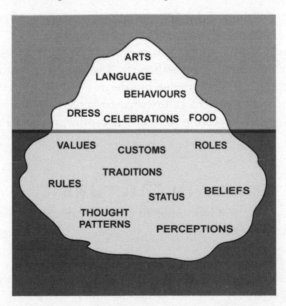

Superficial elements such as language and clothing style are easy to detect—visible to even the most cursory observer. Yet there are a great number of intangibles hidden from view, like common beliefs and values, which exert powerful influences on how crowds and individuals behave. Outsiders unfamiliar with these risk ramming into them unawares when entering a new geography or social community.

SITUATIONAL AWARENESS

Our rule #1 when it comes to Cultural Capital is to develop an accurate awareness of the culture in which you live. Or plan to live, for those of you considering re-locating.

What is the culture of the area in which you live? What do people value? Do you share those values? Will you fit in? And be happy doing so? To what extent do people know and support each other? Will crisis strengthen or weaken that support? In short, is the culture serving you or working against you?

These are important questions to get clarity on, because culture is the only one of the 8 Forms of Capital that you have very little ability to influence directly yourself. In most cases, it's just too widely held amongst too many people for a single individual to make a difference over any meaningful amount of time.

Given that, you pretty much have a stark set of choices when it comes to your surrounding culture: *adapt to it, or move.*

Which is why we encourage you to make an honest assessment of the culture of your community and evaluate how well it fits for your personality, your life aspirations, and your sense of safety.

If you decide your current culture doesn't serve you well enough, then it's time to consider relocating to one that promises a better fit. More on that shortly.

A CASE STUDY IN CULTURE

Here's a good example of how different cultures can behave very differently given the same situation.

New Orleans, 2005

Hurricane Katrina slammed into New Orleans on August 29, 2005, devastating the city. A general evacuation order was issued, but because the storm surge caused the failure of 53 levees, 80% of the city flooded, preventing many citizens from leaving.

In the days that followed, bedlam reigned. Stores were looted (initially by those desperately seeking food and water), and soon more violent crimes like carjacking, murder and rape skyrocketed. Vigilantism spiked in response, as people sought to protect themselves and their property. The city police were soon joined by the National Guard to restore order, resulting in deadly clashes with the populace and rampant reports of law enforcement abuse and misconduct.

Relief supplies were abysmally long in arriving due to terrible mismanagement of the logistics by local authorities, Homeland Security and FEMA. Deaths continued in the days following the hurricane from thirst, exhaustion and violence that better coordination could have avoided.

In the end, the shortcomings of its culture made the destruction in New Orleans much worse than it should have been. Long-simmering race and class divisions within the city erupted when the veneer of civility was washed away in the disaster. People unused to caring for themselves reacted angrily when their normal channels and systems broke down.

The levee system could have been engineered to withstand Katrina's storm surge, but its repair and maintenance had been neglected over the preceding decades as politicians raided the budget for their pet projects. The insular and territorial agencies responsible for responding to such an emergency clearly did not work in close enough partnership, before or during the tragedy.

New Orleans was simply very poor in the kind of Cultural Capital that would have helped it persevere through a crisis like Katrina. Yes, Katrina was a bad hurricane, but the entire blame for the horrible aftermath rests with a failed culture.

Now, contrast this to another, even worse, natural disaster that occurred on the other side of the world just a few years later.

Japan, 2011

On Friday, March 11, 2011, a magnitude 9.0 earthquake struck off the Pacific coast of Tōhoku, Japan. This was the 4th most-powerful earthquake in recorded history.

Felt all throughout Japan, the earthquake created tsunami waves over 100 feet high that flooded coastal regions, travelling as much as 6 miles inland. Over 15,000 people were killed (over seven times Hurricane Katrina's death toll) and over a million buildings were damaged or destroyed. And, famously, three reactors at the Fukushima Daiichi nuclear power plant were destroyed, creating a radioactive crisis in the immediate aftermath of the disaster.

Yet while the loss of life and infrastructure was many times more severe than with Katrina, there were extremely few reports of looting, violence, or crimes of any kind. Police and military personnel were welcomed and provided front-line humanitarian relief. When government resources weren't available, locals banded together to provide for each other. Supplies and services made their way quickly to the many affected regions, and clean up of the devastation happened remarkably quickly.

Much of this calm and effective response demonstrated by the people of Japan was due to values deeply rooted in the culture there. First off, whereas American culture is individualist, Japan's is collectivist—the needs of the group are considered more important than those of the individual. Concepts like *gamen* (enduring deprivation and making sacrifices) and *ganbare* (trying your best, no matter how hard the situation) guided the populace to work together and remain steadfast for the community's sake. A little more of this in New Orleans could have prevented a lot of the chaos that ensued after the levies failed.

We're not trying to glorify Japanese culture over American. Indeed, the passivity with which they accepted the government's media statements did not serve them well during the evasions TEPCO made as it scrambled to deal with the core meltdowns at Fukushima. But we do feel it valuable to demonstrate the extreme degree of difference in response that different cultures can make to the same situation.

Consider the things that you prioritize: career opportunity, living in balance with nature, safety and security—whatever they may be. Ask yourself if the culture where you currently live will serve you in your pursuit. If so, wonderful. If not, it may be time to consider taking action.

FINDING CULTURE THAT SERVES YOU

If you conclude the pervading culture where you live doesn't serve you well, you have two options: make the best of it, or re-locate.

Re-location

Re-locating, obviously, is the more complex of the two and is not to be undertaken lightly. And for some reading this, it may not be feasible currently given family, career, finances or other obligations.

But sometimes, it's the right decision. After concluding that homestead and community resilience will be key factors for prosperity in the future, both Chris and Adam moved their families out of suburbia and into rural areas with high concentrations of small farms and pre-existing appreciation for local sustainability.

It's our personal opinion that many cities are ill-equipped to face the coming future and will be terrible places to live if you value personal safety and freedom from the taxing grind of petty crime. What Katrina visited upon New Orleans, economics has brought down upon Detroit. If we're correct, then a similar fate awaits other major cities, and some of them are barely holding themselves to a civilized standard as it is.

If you're serious about moving to a place better aligned with your attitude and aspirations, start by making a ranked list of what's most important to you in your search. Good ones to consider for your list are:

- Quality of soil
- Climate/length of growing season
- Water availability, access and ownership rights
- Proximity to family/close friends
- State and local tax rates
- Presence of existing community organizations
- Population density
- Proximity to nuclear facilities
- State of local infrastructure (health, transportation, energy, etc)
- Community demographics (what type of people live there?)
- Community psychographics (what do they value?)
- Size and composition of the local economy
- Crime rate

The priorities you settle on will help you create a list of target regions to start investigating. And once you explore them, these priorities will serve as the criteria by which you make your final decision.

But when starting off on this process, address the following question as early as possible: *Do I want to consider leaving the country?* This is very big decision, and in our opinion, while the fantasy appeals to many, expatriating is the right solution for a small minority of people. It takes money and a lot of dedicated effort to assimilate permanently into a foreign society, and there's no guarantee you'll ever be accepted by the locals there as "one of their own."

That said, for the right type of person, moving abroad opens up a wealth of exciting possibilities for resilient living. If you want to explore them, we recommend contacting The Nestmann Group (www.nestmann.com), an international law consultancy based in Arizona that specializes in helping citizens expatriate their assets and/or their families. If you decide you're one of the few better off re-locating to a new country, the founder, Mark Nestmann, and his team can walk you through the process or refer you to other specialists best-suited to your specific needs.

For those choosing to stay domestic but move to a new city or state, we recommend the book *Rawles On Retreats And Relocation* by James Wesley Rawles. While it has a survivalist bent that may not appeal to all, the book is chock full of useful data and assessments—from zoning laws to growing climates to population insights—that will educate you on the benefits and shortcomings of the major geographic regions in the United States.

Once you've zeroed in on a region, we recommend joining Peak Prosperity's **Relocation USA** online group. There, you can ask questions about specific cities and towns within the regions that interest you, and receive first-hand feedback from folks who have lived there.

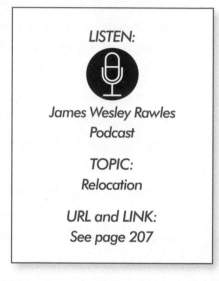

LISTEN:

James Wesley Rawles Podcast

TOPIC:
Relocation

URL and LINK:
See page 207

Making the Best of It

For everyone else planning to stay more or less where they currently are for the foreseeable future, your focus should be on seeking out the sub-cultures that will best foster your future goals.

Every community has sub-cultures. They're the collections of like-minded people who gather, formally or informally, around common ties or interests. Churches, volunteer organizations, athletic clubs, art groups, the regulars at the local bar—all are examples of sub-cultures with their own sets of values, beliefs, traditions, and rules of engagement.

Your mission is to find and join enabling sub-cultures. Which share your values? Which will accelerate your progress in achieving your life goals? Which will best rally to support you in times of crisis?

Chris joined a men's group eight years ago that has served as a tremendously influential sub-culture for him. The group meets bi-weekly, and is designed to help its members surface their challenges and hopes—something rarely allowed by our societal norms, which prefer that conversation remains at a superficial level. The group is designed to keep each participant accountable for making progress with their life goals, offering advice and assistance where it can. The strength and intimacy of the relationships forged in this venue make it one of the most valuable assets in his life today.

Adam has found a similar sense of "family" with CrossFit. For those not familiar with it, CrossFit is a popular fitness program that purposefully cultivates supportive community. Not only has his involvement with CrossFit put Adam into the best physical condition ever, but the friendships made in the gym (or 'box,' for you CrossFitters) have extended into many aspects of his life. Social get-togethers, swapping of professional services, peer-to-peer lending, homesitting, business advising, volunteering together—the support from this sub-culture has been impressively constructive and life-enhancing. At little more than $100 per month, it's one of the highest-return investments he's ever made.

We share our personal experiences to show that sub-cultures come in all shapes and sizes, and oftentimes the full benefits can't be predicted until you jump in with both feet. Our advice is to find a few that look interesting to you, and get involved. If some choices turn out to be disappointments, drop them and move on. But stay active and *participate*—you need to intentionally seek out "your people." They're not going to find their way to you if you don't put yourself out there.

CHANGING CULTURE

Earlier we said that Cultural Capital is the only one of the 8 Forms that the individual can't influence. It turns out that's *mostly* true, but not entirely.

History has plenty of examples of individuals who shaped their culture during their lifetimes: Martin Luther King. Susan B. Anthony. Gandhi. Shakespeare. Hitler. The Beatles. Steve Jobs.

But realistically, few of us will live lives of such immediate and widespread cultural impact.

We can, though, play a role in influencing the evolution of our culture over time. Nobel Prize winning physicist Max Planck famously quipped, "Science advances one funeral at a time," meaning that new ideas advance slowly, and only after those holding the old ones are no longer around to defend them any longer. Similarly, we can contribute to the march of cultural evolution, even though the seeds we plant may not fully bear fruit until after we're gone.

The first way in which we can do this is to live as an example to others. By adopting a resilient lifestyle and demonstrating that quality of life can go up, even as our creature comforts go down, we show the rest of our community that a post-consumption future can be aspired to, versus feared. As humans, we respond to models: We resist making changes until we see others surviving their adoption first. Be one of those trail-blazing early models. It's a win-win: By taking care of yourself first, you inspire others to eventually follow your wise choices, making the community you depend on stronger.

The other way is by teaching our children. Instill the cultural values, beliefs and traditions you think are most valuable. They will live by them and pass that influence along to those they interact with throughout their lives. If enough of us do this, a tipping point will eventually be reached where these elements become the dominant cultural memes.

CHAPTER 13

TIME CAPITAL

Time is our most valuable asset, one that we have less of with each passing moment.

Philosophers of days past kept skulls on their desks as a reminder that their time on earth was short and not to be wasted. While a bit macabre, this was an effective way to maintain the perspective that every moment is sacred and precious, and to be used to its fullest.

But you don't need a skull on your desk if you have children. Growing kids are an effective reminder that time is flying by and that you're getting older. Like all good reminders of the fleeting nature of time, kids let us know that if we have life goals to accomplish, there's no time like the present.

As we've alluded to numerous times each of the steps towards resilience takes time to accomplish, some more than others. For a number of them, it may take a year or more to make real progress.

As you look at the time you have to invest in improving your life—this week, this month, this year—ask yourself: *"How much of it will I budget to spend developing resilience?"* And knowing that there will always be more to do than you have available time, ask next: *"Given that time budget, which steps will I prioritize highest?"*

A SENSE OF URGENCY

As should be crystal clear by now, our work with the Three Es in *The Crash Course* points toward huge changes headed our way. Our economic model is unsustainable and therefore has a crisis (or a set of crises) as part of its very design. In parallel with that, humans are headed towards a very large ecological crisis. Nobody knows exactly when these systems will veer off in a brand new set of directions, but we have a lot of data to suggest this will happen within the next two decades and, once it hits, the pace of change will speed up exponentially.

Truthfully, the various changes predicted in *The Crash Course* have already begun. Change is a process. Whether the eventual change is a small one or a complete collapse, it always is a process instead of a massive sudden "event" like those depicted in so many Hollywood blockbusters.

Peak Oil can be detected in the data showing that the cheap oil deposits are gone. Every new barrel costs $80 or more. Aquifer depletion creeps up on us slowly at first, as wells start needing to be drilled deeper and deeper to reach the water table. Instead of an area running out of groundwater all at once, various farmers individually give up the fight and move away, and slowly people notice that the region is becoming more like a ghost town with each passing year.

We destroy our ecology by a process of a thousand insults, like the various biocides modern farming uses that inadvertently kill off our pollinators, until one day people notice, *Hey! There are no more bees or butterflies around anymore!*

While these kinds of slow, grinding declines happen over many years, they are occasionally punctuated by moments where events accelerate suddenly. This is especially true of human constructs like our financial system, which we last experienced in 2008. One day everything was fine; but then for the next few months, everything was chaos.

Nobody knows exactly when these changes will impact us personally.

Because of this, and because we cannot know if the next big systemic shock will happen tonight or in twenty years, we should act as if it's going to be tonight. Imagine if your entire family slept each night in a house that you knew for sure was going to burn down at some point in the next 20 years.

You might have two decades of safe nights before that happens, or maybe just one more night—the point is, *you don't know*, and that uncertainty would convince a prudent parent to consider moving to a different, safer home. Or at least run fire escape drills with their spouse and children, install smoke detectors and fire extinguishers and test them both regularly, and have some important possessions stored outside of the main house or right by the front door.

But what if we didn't know for *sure*, with 100% certainty, that the house would burn down? What if there was only a 50% chance? How would a prudent person behave then?

This is where we humans tend to get tripped up. While such a high likelihood should absolutely still motivate us towards immediately taking the same prudent steps outlined above, the introduction of probability causes most people to slump back into inaction.

It's the same behavior that explains cigarette smoking. A *chance* of something happening in the future, even if it's as catastrophic as cancer or heart disease, has enough psychological distance to allow people to push those concerns entirely out of daily, conscious consideration. Evolutionarily, we're wired to respond to immediate threats, like the snarling saber-toothed tiger preparing to pounce. We're much worse at dealing with more distant, non-visible threats (climate change, health risks, fiscal recklessness, etc). We tend to discount these risks too much, much to our regret when they eventually manifest.

The good news is that we can overcome this weakness through education and discipline. Monitor the latest developments (that's what we do on a daily basis at PeakProsperity.com). Continually ask yourself what their likely implications are, and what action may be needed on your part in response. And act with a sense of urgency.

If you can do those three things, you'll be much less likely to be caught flat-footed when a sudden correction jolts the world by surprise.

Clear Your Calendar!

The fact that we can't know when the next major jolt will hit, doesn't justify waiting until things become "more clear."

By the time things are obviously bad, a whole new set of factors come into play. For starters, everyone else can now see the danger and will start panicking. Many of the resources you want to procure will become scarce, and your efforts will then be more akin to hoarding than prudent preparation.

So make the time to make resilience-building a priority *now*. Get your schedule out and start reserving room on it for developing the other seven forms of capital. As we mentioned earlier, our initial ask of you is that you commit at least one hour per week over the next three months in order to make this a regular habit in your life.

If you don't, odds are high you'll experience "failure to launch." In our work, we know plenty of well-intentioned people who never get around to actually acting on those intentions. They claim they're just "too busy," but can tell you about every episode of *Game of Thrones* or *Breaking Bad*. These are people who love their children enough to ferry them each week to and from a flurry of sporting events, but who can't find a fraction of that same time to protect their family from possible future harm.

This claim of not having enough time to take the steps recommended in this book is one of the most common excuses we hear, but we know that's not the true reason behind the inaction. Instead, it's that these people aren't yet emotionally ready to confront the prospect of big change.

However, because you've made it this far in the book, we're pretty confident that you're ready and willing to become prepared, resilient, and lead a healthier and happier life, and to join us in working to create a world worth inheriting.

And we're thrilled! The world needs more people like you.

DOING THE NEXT THING

We once visited a woman whose house was an absolute masterpiece of functional beauty. All over her property were mature integrated gardens, abundant supplies of water, blooming fruits and flowers, and solar energy installations—seemingly every corner and crevice of her land bursting with the type of Living and Material Capital most of us would drool over.

When asked how she had managed to find the time to create such a grand opus of function and beauty, such a masterpiece of human effort, the woman simply replied, "*I just did the next thing.*"

That response immediately resonated with us because of the important lesson it contains. Life is a series of small moments and efforts strung together. If done thoughtfully and purposely over time, they compound. Each new one is built on the shoulders of the ones before it, and with perseverance, great accomplishments will result.

Whether we are building our business, developing our gardens, becoming more involved in our community, or improving our homestead, progress happens by a relentless pursuit of "doing the next thing."

Don't get hung up on how big a project is, or how much work remains to be done. Slow and steady wins the race. Remember, this is going to be a marathon, not a sprint. While there may be times you kick things into a higher gear because of world events, or to push a project over its own hillcrest, there's no "done" in this race. There's just "better."

As a society, we're going to spend decades digging out from the various predicaments we've made for ourselves economically, environmentally and especially in our dependence on energy. In light of that, your ongoing progression of "next things" will look like hyper-speed in the eyes of the average Joe.

TAKING CONTROL BY LETTING GO

Many of the things we face are predicaments. Unlike problems, which have solutions, predicaments only have outcomes that need to be managed. We can either attempt to manage those outcomes intelligently, or ignore them and hope for the best. But either way, we'll have to live with the outcomes.

An example of one of the many predicaments we face is the horribly underfunded state our public and private pensions programs—at a time when the cohort of retired workers is expanding rapidly. That's not a problem; it's a predicament.

What has to be managed are the expectations of all those who were promised those pensions. There aren't nearly enough funds today to have a hope of paying those pensions out in full. To address the gap, we'll have to choose either to increase taxes and fees placed on existing workers, or pay retirees lower payments than they were promised. It's simple math—and we'll probably have to end up doing both. And yet companies, municipalities, states and the federal government are all complicit in choosing the "ignore it and hope for the best" strategy.

Of course, that will only make this predicament more painful to address when the issue becomes impossible to ignore.

This is common, sadly. Most people will look at such predicaments and, without the possibility of a solution, give up hope and turn away. But in reality, there are always smart choices to make that will have great influence on how things turn out. We just need to stop feeling powerless and take matters into our own hands.

Using this example, while we as individuals can't change the underfunded nature of the pension funds, we can control our expenditures in anticipation of the looming shortfalls. If we learn to live well at a lower expense level by the time we get to retirement, we'll not feel the bite nearly as badly as an unprepared person if our pension payments are cut (and if they end up paying out at 100%, we'll feel rich!).

Similarly, we can't change how much carbon dioxide the world produces, but we can control our own carbon footprint. None of us have any control over how much new money the Federal Reserve prints up, but we can protect our paper wealth from inflation by investing in tangible assets.

One way to think about this is in terms of a simple two-by-two grid, that puts a bit more substance around the Serenity Prayer authored by American theologian Reinhold Niebuhr:

God, grant me the serenity to accept the things I cannot change,
The courage to change the things I can,
And the wisdom to know the difference.

It's called the Control Continuum:

THE CONTROL CONTINUUM

	CAN CONTROL	CAN'T CONTROL
ACT	**Right Action**	**Ceaseless Striving**
DON'T ACT	**Giving Up**	**Letting Go**

Let's start in the top left corner. When you take prudent steps on the issues you can control, you're taking the **right action**, which is where mastery develops. We can control our own food production and become master gardeners. We can control how socially involved we are and our emotional reaction to stress. By doing so, we are becoming more resilient. This is the quadrant you want to be investing the vast majority of your energies in.

But when you take action on things you can't control (the upper box on the right), this is **ceaseless striving**. You're simply wasting your time and energy. Yelling at the president on the television, silently wishing someone would treat you differently, and fighting for a larger share of the water from a depleting aquifer are all lost causes. This is the quadrant you want to spend the least amount of your time in. Stop doing any activity that you realize is ceaseless striving.

When you do have control over an outcome, but you're *not* taking action, you're down in the lower left quadrant. This is **giving up**. It's where a lot of fear and anxiety live for a great many people. Failing to buy a simple earthquake survival kit when you live near a fault line, letting yourself get out of shape, keeping your investments fully invested in stocks and bonds out of laziness—all are examples of giving up. And even though "doing nothing" sounds easy, it comes with a cost. It takes an emotional toll, because you know you're ignoring responsibility and are putting yourself and those who depend on you at risk. This never sits easy in the psyche. Take a hard look at the things you are avoiding or have on auto-pilot. If the potential cost of neglect could be high for any, move that activity into the **right action** quadrant.

The final box, on the lower right, is when we ignore the things over which we have no control. This is **letting go,** and it, too, is a form of mastery. By accepting the things we cannot change, it doesn't mean we surrender to them, but that we've accepted they're a part of our reality that we can't avoid. We recognize their presence, tweak our plans, and get on with life. This is very psychologically freeing, and opens our minds to creative new ways to take action. Make a list of all of the stresses and frustrations that plague you. How many can you place in this quadrant and simply stop fretting over?

Angry that the central banks (as of the writing of this book) are printing up billions of thin-air money each month and using it to support stock prices? Well, there's nothing you can to change that. But you can move some of your paper cash into tangible assets to protect your purchasing power, or perhaps decrease your exposure to stocks and bonds in defense against a market crash when that bubble pops.

If you identify the issues where you're ceaselessly striving or have given up, and focus your energies as much as possible in the other quadrants, your use of your most precious resource—time—will be vastly improved.

PUT YOUR TIME TO ITS HIGHEST USE

If you're new to resilience building, you'll undoubtedly have to dedicate more time to it than someone who has been at it for a while. This is simply because there's an up front investment in time that pays off over time.

Your authors have spent years in the pursuit of greater resilience. We had to figure out where we wanted to live and move our families there. A good garden takes time to design and years to build up quality soils. Orchards take several years before the trees begin to produce. Raising livestock takes years to figure out how to do properly. Getting fit requires an ongoing investment of discipline. Becoming a trusted and respected member of your community takes many years of repeated interaction with those living around you.

But each type of capital we're building requires less work each year, while the rewards from each grow. The "hard" work is behind us.

That's how it will be for you, as long as you persist. After a few years of **just doing the next thing**, you too will discover that there's a lot less work and a lot more time to sit back and harvest the returns on all your investments.

WHAT SHOULD I DO?

We've mentioned that this is the most common question we're asked. There's no single right answer that applies to everyone.

But as it relates to time, our advice is to use it as wisely as possible to bring you the most joy or the greatest relief. Has it been bugging you that you don't have a 72 hour emergency kit for your family even though you live in an area prone to natural disasters? Then invest the 20 minutes to get one this weekend.

Have you been meaning to get to know your neighbors better and to develop a wider circle of friends and acquaintances? Then host a potluck at your house within the next 30 days.

Feel overwhelmed and you don't know where to start? Then spend an hour just plotting and planning, writing down everything you think you need to do and why. Make a big list. Then rank it according to priority and do the first thing on it.

Our website is full of stories of people just like you who started with a single step, followed by many more, and now have an impressive degree of resilience in their lives.

Here's a particularly relevant one:

> Four years ago we started looking for our homestead.
>
> We were fortunate to live close to some of the most ideal areas in the country for building resilience. Good water, soil, and a large Amish community with their horse powered infrastructure. This area was at the southern edge of the last ice age, giving a good sandy gravel aquifer and well-mineralized soils
>
> We found a 200-year-old brick farmhouse on 12 mostly wooded acres. What sealed the deal was it had a spring room attached to the house with cold clean water running 24 hours a day. The

springs (five of them) are uphill from the house and feed a stream that originates completely on our land.

The house has 12-inch solid brick walls with an outside wood burner and propane backup. The first summer it stayed pretty cool if we opened the windows at night and closed them in the morning but the house was damp.

Our first major investment was a Geothermal heating and cooling system. With the spring water we had an open loop system put in which cooled the house nicely with 55-degree water. The heat drawn out of the air went to heating the domestic water supply. It works well in the winter to heat the house as long as it doesn't get too far below 28 degrees, then the backup propane comes on. With spring water input it supposedly generates $4 of heating and cooling for each $1 of electricity.

Next on the infrastructure list was a bank barn built where the old barn had collapsed. We designed it with a root cellar and a cistern that gravity feeds the livestock tanks in the lower level. The cistern is fed from the roof run off. Float valves in the stock tanks keep the water at level. In hindsight I wish I had also put in an ice room.

Next comes the fencing with tight mesh at the bottom to keep in the chickens and allow them the entire pasture to roam. It is high enough for horses and strong enough for goats. You have to have good fencing when you have six goats! With the goats we have learned to milk, make cheese, and midwife births. It has been fun! The chickens are called Buff Orpingtons and are known to be very social birds who like being picked up and held.

Garden beds are in and fruit trees were planted the first year. More fruit trees and bushes have been added each year. This year we put in the 16 kwh solar panel system while we can still get the tax credit (it expires in 2016). Between it and the Geothermal we are close to being energy independent.

We love this simple life.

What comes across for us in that reader story is the practice of *doing the next thing* and the amount of time it takes to get Material and Living Capital in place. Four years in, and this couple has accomplished a huge amount. They love their simple life, but it took time.

Everyone who writes us tells us they are extremely glad they chose to start down this path, not sure how it would turn out at first. But with the benefit of hindsight, they're firm in their conviction they'd start down it again if given the chance, only sooner.

This next story is of a couple who started ten years ago. With their personal plan largely in place, they're now focusing on inspiring others by creating a teaching homestead:

> Ten years ago we purchased 76 acres in the Texas Hill country. We added a 30,000-gallon rain collection system immediately due to poor quality of the well water and have since increased capacity. We deer fenced (eight feet) a 125' x 125' garden and planted four 125' rows of asparagus plus fruit trees and left space for annual veggies.
>
> We also fenced a 60' x 40' garden closer to the house for Irish potatoes, sweet potatoes and greens and cole crops during the cooler months. We built a root cellar and installed two solar systems (10 kw total). One is a solar system with battery backup, for the cellar and water pumps, and the other a grid tie solar system which has cut our power bill to one-third or less.
>
> We added a pond and packed the bottom with local clay and it has held water quite well, and we have just finished a 40' x 32' x 18' high passive solar greenhouse with thermal chimney cooling and a subterranean heating and cooling air exchange system. It's been kind of like triage, jumping from one project to the other because they are all interlinked, but now we are finally in a phase of finishing details and polishing systems. We also have a wildlife exemption on 50 acres and an agricultural exemption on 26. There are lots of whitetail and axis deer and turkey on our place since we don't hunt. We have four horses and use their manure as the base for our compost which cooks for a year before we use it. We have a guest rental cottage and enjoy showing interested folks what we are doing. Our ultimate goal is to have a functional teaching homestead.

We receive stories like this from readers all the time. We're continuously astonished by what so many of our readers have managed to accomplish. The amount of effort, intelligence, capital and dedication they have poured into their projects is an inspiration to us.

Whether your resilience goals may be more modest or expansive than those reflected in these stories, the main takeaway is this: everything takes *time*.

A handy rule of thumb we've observed is that plans usually take twice as long as anticipated. If you think you might get solar panels installed in six months, plan on a year. Gardens can be created in a year, but really only begin yielding well after a couple of years. Orchards take several years to begin producing, but ten or more to really hit their stride.

Building Emotional and Spiritual Capital is a life-long process, as is adding to your Knowledge Capital. The pursuit of each is never "done," but how far you get with any of them will be a function of how much time you give them.

Everything worthwhile in life takes time. Our invitation is to set goals and set aside as much time as you think is required to achieve them in a realistic manner.

So what should *you* do? We can't answer that for you, specifically, because everyone's situation is different.

But the right time to get started is right now, and when looking at your long list of things that need doing, you should just 'do the next thing.'

READER STORIES

We interspersed several stories within the preceding chapters from our readers at PeakProsperity.com because we can't think of anything that can drive home the points we're making more powerfully than hearing first-hand accounts from real people putting them into implementation in their own lives.

If you're ready to build resilience across the 8 Forms of Capital and are looking for that little extra nudge of inspiration to get started, here are several more stories we didn't have room to squeeze in sooner.

Remember, these are real people, from all walks of life, all ages, all socio-economic backgrounds. Like you, they cared enough to educate themselves about the Three E trends shaping our future, and with that insight, decided it was time to take prudent action in their lives. Some have been able to do a lot; some are just getting started.

But the point is that each is doing what they can. That's all you should be asking of yourself.

C.B.

My wife Patty and I lived in a major metropolitan area in central Florida for a number of decades. After having raised our children and growing tired of the heat we decided to move north. Added to this was an inner feeling we had that society was subtly changing, things were getting more complicated, the food and distribution networks that we all rely on were becoming more susceptible to systemic shock.

We thought long and hard about what and how everything was connected, our quality of life and what we really wanted in our 50s and going forward into our later years. I was in the technology arena, my wife in the construction management industry and she had a fair amount of public service with massage therapy and the "soft arts" so to speak.

As we thought more about this, we realized we really didn't want to be in a city anymore, especially in an area where it seemed people were constantly accelerating their lives, they were mean and nasty and getting more so. Add to this our uneasy feeling that as Peak Prosperity says "the next 20 years are going to be much different than the last 20 years," yet we didn't really understand 36 short months ago what the possibilities were. We just understood that we needed to make a move out to a rural area.

We decided to move to the mountains of North Carolina. After many months shopping for a homestead on a budget (not easy, I saw every nasty, moldy foreclosure in three counties!) we fell into a functional home on a beautiful 15-acre tract that has two running streams, one of them with a source within 50 yards of our property, so it's clean and fresh.

With about five acres in pasture (unusual in the mountains) and the balance in woods, we felt this was a place we can really work on and call home for the long run. I enjoy working outside, and my wife as well, on those things she's picked up along the way. She is a super "help-mate" and I for her as well—we're a good team!

On the property when we arrived was simply a small one sided livestock lean-to and a 2,100-square-foot off-frame modular house—about 10 years old, it was in great shape with a little bit of deferred maintenance. We had to throw some money into the maintenance issues, and a lot of elbow grease, we started to develop a "survival plan" to increase our chances for future comfort and resiliency.

On a shoestring, we started to systematically liquidate a rental property, our 401(k)s and some savings, turning all of it into developing resiliency for the long run for ourselves and our family (not that any of them seem to paying much attention to the issues at hand...).

I fenced in five and a half acres, we purchased a handful of Boer meat goats and started breeding them two years ago. This year for the first time, we had a dozen babies and actually put 150 pounds of goat meat (from last year's crop) in the freezer, yay!

We also put in place three or four raised beds, Patty started doing straw bale gardening with great success, and we also are working on a larger garden. Patty learned canning and "puts up" some great stuff. We supplement that with a couple of "Aero-Ponic" garden towers, which have been tremendously successful in avoiding disease and insects, we even had fresh salad lettuce and assorted greens and herbs throughout last winter (a test) with a small greenhouse we put up about a year ago from Shelter Logic.

Also on the subject of protein, we built a small pole barn 9' x 15' to "test out" raising white New Zealand rabbits. Six cages and we started a breeding program learning to care for these animals last fall.

We've been poking along with it now for about 10 months and have had only one litter, but we're ready to process the first ones here in about three or four weeks, and are now thinking about starting to supplement our "technology" base income with a meat rabbit operation—maybe 20 to 30 does to start with. This will take a larger barn and we're looking into that now. This will also call for an FDA-approved processing facility so we can sell the meat to the public—not all that complicated, it will probably be a small 12 foot by 8 foot shed with the proper requirements.

Also two years ago Patty had always wanted to do beekeeping so she started that out and she's grown from one hive to four hives this year with a good harvest of money last year.

Early on about a year into it we incorporated an 80-hen chicken house, building it under the back of our house, utilizing the deck as a ceiling and building to avoid predators. It works great and we have fresh eggs that we sell around town and have harvested some of our own chickens using YouTube videos. You can learn anything on YouTube!

We are also contemplating a couple of more revenue pillars here, one of which will probably be raising livestock guardian dogs—we love these animals and would like to share them with the world.

Additionally, we are going to be "bottling up" what we've done here in the last 36 months and rolling out our own unique brand of self-reliant/resiliency workshops "on property" for others to learn from us how we've done this and that they can do it too!

We also put in a number of off grid features and functionality, it would be very difficult living without power but at least we would have the basics—food and water.

I'd like to thank Peak Prosperity and Chris Martenson's early videos about the economy and environment etc. much of this was what drove us to do more research and understand the risks and the need for self resilience and increasing our ability to provide for ourselves on an ever (now) accelerating basis.

Hopefully others will take heart, the first step is always the hardest—you must realize if you lived like us, that life was not what it seems, and you just simply need to leave town, go to a new place, either find a job or get involved in something that you can do on a part-time basis or perhaps band together with others. There's a new paradigm occurring as most of us know, and it's not always comfortable, but you have to drive yourself to be goal oriented and hit those objectives as quickly as possible so that at least you have food water and shelter.

We'd be glad to field questions, just let me know how we can be of service to enlighten others to move forward!

W.D.

In 2007, at the age of 52, I got my degree in safety engineering and my base pay went up to $80K a year. With overtime pushing that to $100K, and I still was not making enough to live in the NYC area. I loved my profession, yet I was miserable because I was working 60-hour weeks, with 20 hours of commuting. And I was very worried about the economy; I'd seen in the '70s what a downturn could do to the city. As a futurist and part-time science fiction editor, I saw so many converging negatives: resource depletion, overpopulation, factory farming, antibiotic resistance, aquifer depletion . . . I decided I had to leave the overpopulated area. In the event of a disaster like a Carrington Event or a currency crash, with eight million people plus as many surrounding the city, the greater NY area would be a death trap.

Then the 2008 crash hit, which intensified my decision to move. Had I not met someone with the same concerns, I would have moved to the Midwest, but I met a man with the same non-consumerist lifestyle and concerns. In 2009 I married him, moved to SC, and joined Peak Prosperity. He had a paid off house, and land for a big kitchen garden. He put his retirement monies all in cash. I took the tax hit to use up my IRA to make our home as resilient as possible.

We insulated the house (including window shades), added solar-powered attic fans, a few solar panels, and repaired his solar hot water. We put in an airtight wood burning stove and a skylight for a dark indoor area. We put in a large raised-bed garden, edible landscaping, and planted fruit and nut trees. We put in a well, water- and electricity-saving appliances, and installed screen doors and repaired or replaced window screens, and built emergency supplies. Some of our preps were skills: I got a CCP and became a master gardener and studied permaculture. We learned to can and dehydrate food. We made a point of meeting our neighbors and helped my son move here, where he plugged into the local society by marrying the daughter of a sheriff. We joined a local church where the members take care of one another. As each one of these things was accomplished, we felt more secure about an uncertain future.

Are we in a perfect place to handle things if TSHTF? No: we could use more land, and the area is a little too populous, but I'm worlds better off than I was in NY. We are on the edge of farm country and surrounded by people who are courteous and pretty much share the same self-reliant values. If the power goes out or the banks close we are light-years ahead of our neighbors.

M.D.

My wife and I made the decision to leave the city and find a homestead four years ago. We enjoyed only weekends for two years before moving here full time. Our site selection criteria included a location with a maximum of 70 miles out of the city (metro Nashville, TN). Abundant water resources, timber, and acreage for planting and livestock were essential requirements. God's providence led us to a restored 1920's era home on seven acres. Since our initial purchase, we have added an apple orchard of 70 trees, now producing prolifically, two garden plots that total at least an acre, and two chicken coops with a total of 80 layers.

We drilled a well that provides wonderful fresh water to supplement our city, spring, and stream supplied waters. My wife has become an accomplished soap maker and canner putting up at least 200 jars of vegetables last year and crafting several hundred bars of soap from nearly a dozen recipes.

Additionally, we made contact with the landowner of the adjacent property, which turned out to be the heirs of the original farm and were able to purchase the entire additional 170 acres and reconstitute the farm as it originally stood. Currently, we are in the process of restoring the main hay barn to its original configuration and design. A nearby milk house, long abandoned, is being restored with the intention of establishing a "community store" for us to sell our produce, eggs, and soaps. We intend to make the space available to anyone in the community to bring their crafts for sale or trade. We are excited about the unfolding possibilities. One neighbor has already committed to providing restoration expertise and will be adding iron work crafts, hand-crafted syrups, honey, and additional vegetables. We feel, at this point, the possibilities are endless.

P.W.

It all started with Hurricane Katrina. Before her, I was blissfully unaware. It was the summer of 2005, and my wife, Denise, and I just closed on a 1.4 million dollar McMansion, 30 minutes outside of Washington D.C. The housing bubble was in full swing, although it wasn't being called a bubble. You were more apt to hear, "They can't make any more land."

When Katrina hit the Gulf Coast, it caused a shortage of gasoline and diesel in the Northeast. As the owner of a landscape design and maintenance firm, this concerned me. I wondered, *How could a storm in the Gulf cause shortages in Virginia?* During the storm, I did what most people do when they're concerned about the supply of a vital resource: I hoarded. I instructed my guys to fill up their trucks and their equipment. We bought a hundred extra gas cans and filled them up, too. I knew without diesel and gasoline, my crews couldn't operate, and if my crews couldn't operate, we would be hemorrhaging money, as fixed expenses and salaries would still need to be paid.

A few weeks later, business was back to normal, and fuel was more expensive, but never unobtainable. I was relieved to weather the storm, so to speak, but my original question gnawed at me. How could a storm in the Gulf cause shortages in Virginia? I started researching the oil market, so I could better position my business in the future. Where does our fuel come from?

How much of it do we have? How secure is it? Are there viable alternatives? The information I came across was sobering, and I didn't want to believe it, because if what I was reading was true, my business, my way of life, was completely unsustainable. I searched for information that soothed my worry.

I searched for information that said, "There's nothing to worry about, everything's fine. Keep doing what you're doing."

I wanted to believe the cornucopians, as they were called, that talked of hundreds of years of abundant oil. Deep down, I knew they lacked something. They lacked the data. If you analyzed the data, it was simple.

At the time, I was the envy of family and friends. I was 29 years old, with a large salary, and a larger house. I started to question what I was doing. Was I making the world a better place or was I just contributing to our hyper-consumptive materialistic culture? I knew the answer, but it was hard to face. My business burnt copious amounts of precious non-renewable fuel to maintain landscapes in an artificial state of immaturity. We sprayed chemicals; we planted useless ornamentals, and contributed to the 'keeping up with the Joneses' mentality that's so pervasive in the suburbs. My personal life wasn't much better. I had inefficient cars, a house that was way too big for two people, and I didn't know how to do anything practical.

I wanted out. I wanted out of the consumerist lifestyle: the McMansion, the cars, the business, all of it. I wanted to live a more self-sufficient, self-reliant lifestyle, where I felt like I was part of the solution. Denise and I had many late night discussions of what we should do.

Ultimately, we agreed to sell everything. It took five months to sell the house, my business, and the cars. At the end of those five months, with the weight of debt and responsibilities removed, I felt…free.

With no jobs and no responsibilities, Denise and I traveled up and down the east coast searching for a sustainable place to settle. We were expecting to find quaint small towns with beautiful countryside and farms. What we found were strip malls, fast food joints, and a degraded landscape that looks very much the same wherever we went. The farms that we see on marketing at grocery stores were not the reality of the chem-ag monoculture that we saw in the countryside. We never did find that healthy, sustainable, environment we were looking for. We settled for rural Central Pennsylvania, where the soil was good and the town wasn't too commercialized.

We purchased a six-acre hayfield, and built a simple, but super-efficient home made from insulated concrete that produces twice the energy it uses. We live simply and debt free.

Over the next seven years, I got my hands dirty, turning our old hayfield into a homestead that can provide for our needs. I learned all the things long since forgotten and deemed useless in our society. I learned to grow fruits and vegetables, animal husbandry, beekeeping, green building, alternative energy, and permaculture design. Denise went back to teaching, where she became a state teacher of the year finalist, and a college professor. In the summer she's a huge help in the fields and in the kitchen.

My former life seems like a lifetime ago. As a permaculture designer and consultant, I make a fraction of what I once did, but all of my endeavors are clearly on the solutions side as I help others to design and implement regenerative permaculture gardens and farms. As a homesteader, with my own permaculture site, it is a soul-satisfying endeavor to produce abundant healthy food of the highest quality. We've transformed our property with 2,000 linear feet of swales, 1,500 multifunctional trees and shrubs, four ponds, 70 linear feet of hugelkultur berms, hundreds of pounds of seed, and many tons of compost and mulch. Seven years ago it was a degraded hillside cut for hay; now it is an interconnected, dynamic ecosystem brimming with life. This land, this home, will be here providing for the needs of its inhabitants long after we're gone.

K.K.

Back in high school in the late '70s, in geography class I wrote a thesis on IMF, the World Bank and debt slavery and in biology class I conducted a scientific experiment and wrote a thesis on the effects of environmental imbalances for small ocean crustaceans. A couple of years ago I wrote a blog entry titled "Fucked…with a twist" where I recalled a spontaneous visualization I did with one of my friends, also during high school, where we imagined what our living conditions would be like in the case of a real shortage of oil.

Actually I am of an optimistic temperament, so this introduction is just to say that this knowledge, these visions of the imbalances and potential harsh consequences of our current way of life, have been a faithful companion all through my life. I educated myself as an architect, drew up my first proposal for a zero energy house, and I further educated myself within the field of energy-saving and environmentally friendly architectural practices and held positions within this field on various architectural offices, but the position was hardly ever more than a kind of flagging of good intentions.

And I have been doing lots of community work, developed transitional skills, taken full responsibility for my personal well being, made daring new career steps, and yet the story I want to tell is a complicated and demanding one, and it has to do with the potential of images, of art, of architecture, to challenge the way we perceive ourselves in relation to our surrounding world.

In the spring of 2009 the Italian clothing manufacturer Benetton, known for its multicultural and barrier-breaking societal stance, invited architects all around the world to submit proposals for two office buildings in Tehran. This was during "The Persian Spring" which actually preceded The Arab Spring. And I went to Tehran and studied the architecture of the city and submitted a proposal, which incorporated four different architectural motifs, both local and international, which were prevalent in the city.

The whole point of this eclectic approach was to raise the question of identity, what are the functions of identity in our personal lives and in our societal narratives? And my point was, that a crucial aspect in changing the way we behave, in changing the way we constantly limit ourselves and creates conflicts in our relations has to do with a habit of setting up far too constricting identities for ourselves. The architectural design was a probe into a representation of a multifaceted identity.

As a matter of fact, we are all multifaceted beings. Thus the design is an invitation to loosen up yourself, and allow other people to be who they are and to have their own perspectives and preferences. Just as the façade of the proposal, we might think of our identities as dynamic semi-permeable membranes through which we are able to constantly exchange ideas and inspirations with our surroundings. Open Source as a state of being.

C.D.

It was hearing Peter Schiff being interviewed on NPR that woke me up in 2007.

I wandered on to *The Crash Course* a bit after that. I moved to Vermont from downtown Boston and set up an online company distributing Vermont-made products nationally.

The building came with part ownership of a 200-gallon-per-minute mineral spring whose overflow had powered a 24-foot waterwheel behind our building. (We're setting up a hydro-power project next.)

Over time we did quite a few things:
• Added 86 solar panels
• Solar hot water

- Rooftop spring-fed vegetable gardens
- Interior wood-fired boilers for heat and hot water

A few years ago I bought a neighboring two-acre 1700's colonial and moved my friends Marc and Lisa onto it to start a micro-farm. Marc lived in Moldovia during the collapse of the Soviet Union and worked in a chicken processing plant there during that time. My deal with them was to come be my tenant/neighbor and I'd invest my capital in setting up a farm for them.

I also bought more of my neighbors' houses as they moved and set them up as Vermont vacation rentals. However they also double as housing for my extended family, if things in the world go off the rails.

We basically have a compound with everything we need for years of hiding in plain sight. Also a lot of this is what we got off your site postings. Love what you do. Keep up the good work

R.H.

I offer my story for diversity purposes and to offer encouragement for those that need it. As well for those at the emotional beginning that may not have the outward physical changes reflecting the internal changes in development.

Beginning in 2007, six months before the plunge in housing, we purchased our home that stretched our income-to-mortgage ratio to over 30%, just because the bank told us we could. And also because we were following culture's set of values and not our own. If you had asked me then I would have denied it! My ego was very active as was my male testosterone-driven sense of self.

The years 2007and 2008 turned out to be a significant time of self-evaluation and awakening, stripping away of the fragile shell of culture for which I found my self worth. Before I was able to manifest any physical changes resembling resilience I first had to approach a head full of nonsense, and a consumer-driven lifestyle lacking direction or purpose.

My first steps were watching *The Crash Course* on DVD and reading Charles Eisenstein. (Everything he writes or says, but mostly it was *Ascent of Humanity* that helped the most). I then followed that up with many internal experiences for neurological re-wiring, and re-educating which the major players of that being, new found friendships through fully present experiences, men's group, music, meditation and entheogenic medicine. All of which provided much needed comfort, emotional uplift, insight, and strength. This was done by intention and under the wing of one of the most beautiful and well-practiced humans beings I have ever had the grace of sharing space with. I don't recommend doing it without this sort of presence.

After seven years in this unsustainable mortgage, we made our break leaving behind our savings in the upside-down mortgage it would have taken 14 years to get out of. Moving three times in one year, we eventually were able to buy a much smaller house at half the mortgage on a lot four times as large. Now we have a large backyard garden, compost, a coop full of chickens, a new self-remodeled house. All of which are creating many newly formed skills and increased self-confidence. Built upon a complete neurological upgrade intended for resilience and personal growth. All of my projects are done on budget and completed in time spent after work and during weekend hours. Which often means resourcing from unlikely places and materials or just plain waiting until the project can be afforded. Most often it's the available resources choosing the project, rather than my act of choosing. I won't go too much into the details of the physical manifestations of my work because most of the effort for me is on the emotional resilience side, which I find much more compelling.

It is never too late to change yourself and if you're like me, especially at the early stages, it can all seem so impossible to tackle, because the changes feel too big and numerous and the world to foreign. The important thing I came to understand is nobody pulls themselves up by their own bootstraps. Everyone requires help, and its always closer and more accessible than you feel it is. Especially when you start asking and offering without shame. This is why my successes and failures are intimately linked and often confused. A good friend of mine would say "My answers have now become questions and my questions answers." I have found my advantages are increased creativity, innovation and having something that is completely unique and debt free creating a wealth/skill all its own. I'm not pressed to make more money only free up more time in which to experience life's many bipolar unfoldings.

C.W.

We were living in the sustainable urban community of Takoma Park, MD when research for my job brought me across *The Crash Course* and, then, to what became the Peak Prosperity on-line community.

Our house in Takoma Park was outfitted to the best of our sustainable resilient/abilities complemented by many applicable municipal services but our appreciation of evolving circumstances was constantly enhanced by Peak Prosperity and attendance at a retreat hosted by Chris, Becca, and Adam. Our minds and imaginations had become fertile ground.

A friend had told Meg about Broomgrass after meeting the founders at a Maryland Green Festival and so when Meg and I found ourselves in Berkeley Springs, WV for a birthday celebration, we decided to spent a couple of hours touring the property with Lisa, one of the founders. Meg and I didn't have to say a word. We looked at each other as we departed, and a glance and a shrug told us we were about to embark on a new path.

We had visited a 320-acre, communally owned working organic farm nestled in the Shenandoah Valley less than two hours from Washington, D.C. and Baltimore; 16 one-acre lots owned by individual residents, 304 acres owned and managed by the community. So far, there are chickens (broilers and layers), a small cattle herd, hops, barley, corn, bees, and even a commercial hay operation. There is a large community, deer-fenced garden, but each household typically sports a robust garden. We own a barn and extensive equipment, and any resident can contribute a project as part of the "farm plan" at any community meeting. Plus, Broomgrass is situated in a rich agricultural valley and surrounded by a robust CSA (Community Supported Agriculture) network of farms.

Being life-long urban, suburban dwellers, Meg and I will be advancing a plan to "farm energy" by capitalizing solar panels on the barn to provide energy back for partial operations. As I write this today, our quarterly meeting is being held and one resident proposed a small passel of hogs to move in rotating forest-based paddocks. Meg and I are considering trying an acre or so with oats, then corn, to derive two annual harvests.

We sold our house in Takoma Park and that financed our buy-in and the building of our home here. Lisa and her husband Matthew are the founders; both are young, innovative, preservation specialist LEED-certified architects and Lisa designed and help build our house. All homes must be geothermal, use an approved well and septic system, and house all HVAC systems internally. Ours will get solar as the finishing touch—we made the move April 1, 2015—a propitious day, eh?

The value of this story is that there are entire communities evolving driven by the tenets that Peak Prosperity pioneers, evolves, and advances. Matthew and Lisa did extensive research and legal and financial exploration to structure the best tax and preservation options for a sustainable agricultural community.

As one might imagine, there are many avenues to take in a discussion of this new experiment—especially as the community grows. Right now, there are seven homes, five year-round households, two original lots for sale, and two or three lots for resale as owner's have changed their life plans.

Dramatic changes require many adjustments. Livelihood, relationships, family, and many considerations loom when making life transitions. Shoot, think of Chris's own story and Becca's initial thoughts.

Chris, Becca, Adam, Peak Prosperity, and the PP community stimulate thought, advance possibilities, and suggest solutions in the framework that Chris explores, analyzes, and dissects. Thanks Chris, et al. The adventure continues…

C.R.

We began to understand the scope of the problems after 9/11. My husband Marc had just started a new job at AT&T in New Jersey. Fast-forward about two years and Marc quit because he was asked to increase his security clearance. This meant NSA work and he didn't want that. Marc got a new job, we moved to Somerville, MA, and I left my hometown of NYC and transitioned to working freelance. We were ready for a change—the Iraq War had started and I felt numbed by how unconcerned people seemed.

But Marc was let go after less than a year, and I was pregnant. I couldn't imagine continuing to get new jobs and moving wherever they told us to. We started home-based businesses: Marc is a speech technology consultant and I am a medical writer. We needed a place where we could live on less income. So we moved to Seattle, where Marc owned a house.

Parenthood is hard. Our son was born with so much spirit our world shifted on its axis. On top of this strain, I went back to school to study public health. We were almost unbearably busy and overwhelmed. We were coming to understand the interconnected "3E" story, but lacked the time to truly prepare beyond food storage and purchasing some gold.

Also, we were not a social success in Seattle. We were learning dire things; people thought we had extreme opinions. We lost some friends. It was a very emotional time, full of frustration and a sense of loss.

But we also made some friends. For example, Marc met Michael; they were both former Mormons and had a lot in common. Michael is a handyman, and eventually he became our roommate. He doesn't pay rent, but he fixes things, and helps with cooking and cleaning. It usually works well.

After 10 years, when there was no more we could do, fix, or grow at our home, it was time to leave Seattle. We wanted land and a place with a stronger sense of community. We moved to Vashon, a 37-square-mile island on the Puget Sound between West Seattle and Tacoma. It's only accessible by a 20-minute ferry ride. We got here in September 2013 and bought a beautiful place on eight acres. It's divided into four lots, so we have the flexibility to build, and it's set up for agriculture.

Things really started rolling late last year when Michael and I took a two-week Permaculture Design Course (PDC) on Vashon. It was run using gift economy, and I met my new local tribe. Here's just one story of how life has changed: A new PDC friend had a pregnant cow, but no pasture. We had a pasture. So we entered into a cow-share relationship, and now we share a cow and a calf. We also have chickens, goats, and a big new garden.

Related to our jobs, it took a while, but Marc and I are successfully self-employed. We work virtually, with very low overhead, with several income streams. Our extended family now includes our second son, my biological mother, and friends—new and old—who are making our home theirs for at least part of the year. They are helping us turn this into a sustainable place and hopefully a small community.

I spend a lot of time thinking about how Americans will live together in the future—we're a nation of failed communal living experiments, so what will we do when we are forced to cooperate? These days, I think of my current life as a real-world workshop on communication issues important to our next (probably downscaled) iteration.

To close, I'll say that everyone in our family is on a sharp learning curve. It is exhausting and stressful, but there is also a lot of joy. There's no way to come to terms with these issues without learning something about gratitude. I'm very grateful.

D.H.

My journey down this path began early. I was born in the early '70s and seemed to pick up on the environmental and energy concerns of that decade. My father would say such things as, "Use all the lights you need, but if you aren't using them turn them OFF." These ideas became my baseline understanding of the world.

Early on my goal was to be an artist for a living. I was realistic enough to expect many lean years of income with this career choice, and I would probably never be rich. So I planned from the beginning to keep my cost of living low, and where possible, direct my spending toward lowering future expenses.

I bought my home while still in college. I actually feel a bit sorry for my realtor who spent two years helping me find the place. His commission was very small because I was looking at the lowest-priced properties available. What I bought was a small, old mobile home on 1.5 acres in a rural setting. My monthly mortgage payment was significantly less than the average monthly rent at the time. I worked hard to pay it off in nine years, thus eliminating my largest monthly bill.

Along the way I invested what I could in transforming the thermal nightmare that was the mobile home into an energy efficient abode. This involved the normal things of new windows, efficient lighting, etc. It also involved less normal modifications. I built a shell around it to form an attic and 12-inch thick walls creating the space needed to super insulate.

Another major project was creating a small passive solar, earth-sheltered building. Primarily this was to be my art studio, but it also doubles as a storm shelter. It became a project for learning how to put together a small photovoltaic system. Recently I was able to get a second, larger, off-grid photovoltaic system installed to power my whole home, eliminating another monthly bill.

I started gardening as soon as I moved to this property, slowly learning and expanding my abilities. I installed a couple 1,500-gallon cisterns to collect rainwater mostly for garden use, but also as a backup water supply if needed. Lately I've been working to establish more edible perennial plants/trees. I should also note that I spent a couple years learning about edible wild plants in my region, especially those that grow on my property.

I did achieve my goal of becoming a professional studio artist. As expected, there were many very lean income years. Even now as a "successful" artist my income just barely qualifies for middle class. I think I still fall short some years. However, due to my efforts to create a low cost of living, and investing in things that lower my future expenses, I have an extremely high quality of life. Money hasn't been a real concern for many years now. I may not make huge sums, but what I do amply meets my needs.

I didn't set out to live a more environmentally friendly life. Nor did I start down this path in fear of a major economic collapse. Yet I discovered that living a lower-impact lifestyle saves money as well as environmental resources, and offers me more resilience as our economies decline. All the while I've been increasingly empowered to direct my time, and live my life, as I desire.

J.M.

We came to homesteading from two different angles. Becky, my partner, was a nurse practitioner for 27 years in metro Boston. In 2012, she left suburbia and bought a farm in western Massachusetts, surprising even herself with this decision. The farm is called "OMG Farm" short for "one more gamble." Becky had grown increasingly appalled at the broken industrial food system in America as she treated patients, and she envisioned growing as much of her own food as possible, because of the obvious health benefits compared to a conventional diet.

By the time I met Becky in 2012, I had several years of obsessive reading under my belt, ranging from Dmitry Orlov to Joel Salatin, to Wendell Berry. I had decided that I wanted to try my hand at a small-scale beef herd, and to start doing more things that had real-world practicality instead of the more abstract things that have earned me a paycheck.

I think it's accurate to say that Becky came at homesteading from more of a positive angle—things like making local connections, learning about growing food and permaculture. My motivation was more out of a desire to be better prepared for some systemic failure that I felt was bound to happen. (This sounds like a joke but it's true—Jared Diamond's book, *Collapse*, rested on my bedside table for almost a year.)

So about two years ago, I got six cows and Becky was kind enough to invite them to live on her farm. She invited me to live at the farm, too, but not for another year or so. I also helped get some bees set up on the farm (I wrote the "Beginning Beekeeping" article on the Peak Prosperity site, and this is a major love of mine.)

Some things we share:
- A fascination with natural systems and low-input farming (ask me about dung beetles!)
- Creativity and repurposing
- Paying attention and taking time to observe what's happening on the farm
- Most of all, I think we both value simplicity and desire a simpler life—we fuel our masonry heater with wood cut here.

So both of us have made the choice to work part-time, and use this extra time for things agricultural. We've made several attempts at repurposed structures: last winter's hay-bale chicken house, while not an abiding structure, fulfilled its design goal. I'm planning a simple lean-to for my now-larger herd to use as a winter shelter, exploring ways to reduce the hay bill, and actively trying to use grazing to improve the pastures and increase fertility and productivity. Becky has done an amazing job with the garden and a huge variety of fruit and nut trees.

On my day off (when I'm not at the part-time job) I typically work 10 or 12 hours, do a lot of brush cutting, scything, and fencing. I watch cows a lot, too. It's great for blood pressure. I have an awesome farmer's tan, and have never felt happier. Even more important, I think my focus has shifted from waiting all the time for some big shoe to drop to appreciating the amazingly rich life I have here with Becky.

G.D.

About 20 years ago I was unemployed and easily qualified for the government assistance I depended on to feed my daughter. After a certain amount of desperation and help from Robert

Kiyosaki's books, I learned about the financial rules that we all live under in this country. I learned how to arrange my affairs within these rules to keep more of what I earned. Long story short, I ended up making a good living in the San Francisco Bay Area in the technology industry. I married an attorney that worked at a prestigious law firm in downtown San Francisco. With my new-found wealth, I bought expensive cars, expensive home theaters, expensive vacations, expensive dinners and expensive hair-cuts. I was deep in debt and really living paycheck to paycheck. I was working long hours and playing hard because I felt I deserved it.

Once I learned about the problem with our society's "Three Es," I realized how unsustainable my lifestyle had become. I was happy that I finally had money in my life, but what I really wanted was financial security. I learned that if I saved 10% of my income per year I would need to work 10 years to take one year off. I made a plan to save 70% per year and work only if I choose to. First goal was to pay off all debt with the ultimate goal being no monthly payment commitments on anything. My wife and I sold our German luxury cars and bought sensible cars for cash. We canceled cable TV and all unnecessary monthly bills. We paid off all our loans except our house and her student loans.

The second goal was to get our lifestyle in order. We had suddenly realized how much stuff we had collected and made plans to reduce the amount of stuff we owned. We sold only the most expensive items, the rest we donated. We donated lots of stuff, dozens of car loads to the local Goodwill. We reduced the amount of our belongings so much that we could now move from a 2,400-square foot home in San Francisco to a 500-square foot mobile home in a trailer park 15 miles south.

The move drastically reduced my cost of living and after the move, I only needed 30% of my net income to live, the rest I invested and saved. After watching a few documentaries on the difficulty of making ends meet after retirement, my wife and I set a plan to be secure in our retirement. We assumed we would not get anything back from what we've paid into Social Security, but the hard part here was not knowing what the economy will be like in the future.

We dare not depend on a return from any single investment, so we diversified. We bought several investment properties in a different state. My partner and I grew our business substantially while I also regularly bought gold. Now the risk of having a retirement income is split between a small business, tax-deferred retirement accounts (cash), Social Security income, gold, and real estate.

My lower cost of living, and the security of having several potential sources of retirement income, has made both my wife and me feel secure enough to seek out new careers. We both made plans with our jobs to work far fewer hours. With meaningful help from Adam's book *Finding Your Authentic Career*, I now spend at least three full days per week working on alternative fuel ideas for combustion engines.

I know there's much more that can be improved with my finances. Each month I must pay rent, I must pay utilities, I'm exposed to bank account confiscation, and more. But I couldn't be happier with my progress and I'm proud of my new-found freedom. Even with a completely off-grid Earth Ship, financial resilience is a requirement for happiness.

K.

I was raised on a dairy farm in New Jersey. Had the life, but didn't know it. Left at age 13 with Mom and stepfather. Enter the world of the DC area and fast food, both parents working and leading the good life, so to speak. No more milking cows, gathering eggs, baling hay, driving the tractor, tending the garden....all that hard work that no one really likes to do!

I am now a 64-year-old female still living in the DC area, going about my every day life: get up, go to work, sit all day, come home, sit and watch TV. One day, my son and daughter-in-law asked me to take the self-assessment that was on the PeakProsperity.com website. So I said, "Sure." The first time I filled it out, I disliked it so much, I actually threw it away after filling out the first page. It made me feel very uncomfortable to the point that my stomach got upset. Some weeks later, it popped up in my mind, and I tried it again. This time I got a little further, but that uneasy feeling came back, and again I threw it away.

It kept bothering me that I could not seem to be adult enough to finish it. Once more I took it. This time I got through most of it, but again grew tired of it and filed it away in a book. About a week later, I took it out of the book and decided I was going to finish it and I did. A little later the same day, I erased my answers and took it again. And I took it again until not only did it not send shivers down my spine and upset my stomach, but I felt that I was empowered by taking it.

I read Peak Prosperity most days, listen to Survival podcasts, don't watch TV, and spend most of my waking time (when not at work) outside in a small garden, growing herbs and vegetables. I have a compost bin as well. Have to give the credit to my kids as they implemented it for me. I have some canned food stored and would like to continue to build this lifestyle. Most of my friends don't even want to discuss what I do and they think I am crazy. They shop, get their hair and nails done and make payments on huge credit card debt.

I look forward to retirement in two years, when I can sell my four-bedroom home and move to some land with a few chickens or ducks, a huge garden along with a water source and an outdoor kitchen. I am a single person, which makes the financial part of my life a little bit more difficult, but I am financially free and I know I will continue to be that way. Thank you.

J.S.

We've led a blessed life. In 2005, as our youngest was visiting colleges, we discovered that another was on the way. This was our first experience in being confronted with truly unexpected change. It went swimmingly and our baby brought chaotic joy while our newly empty-nest friends flitted off to the islands. Life was still very much the idyllic American Dream. Our careers as a lawyer and an advertising writer were fun and rewarding. We loved our home, our friends and family, our leisure, our work—everything. Sure, the economy was sometimes weird, but this was America, so we didn't worry at all.

Oddly, neither of us can recall a moment, incident, or situation that led us to take note of anything asunder. All we recall is my husband (not a shopper, ever), running to a couple of milk crates' worth of Dinty Moore Beef Stew®, canned mac and cheese, tuna (of course), jam, Spaghettios… you get the idea. He said, "This is in case we have an emergency." We felt invincible as we placed those crates into the closet of one of our grown kids' abandoned bedrooms. We still laugh about that night.

Random, but so real—it was the night our life's direction was forever changed.

Soon, in an equally strange blur that we can't define, perhaps providence, we found ourselves looking at remote properties in our state. We started tracking credible commentaries and advice from Peak Prosperity and digging like kindergartners into fiscal policies, politicians, agendas and economics. We felt like we were starting a new line of tin foil hats. We challenged ourselves at every turn "Should we stop this nonsense? Have we lost our minds? Would we feel better if we just stopped all of this time and resource-intense activity?" Not once could either of us say "yes," and each week seemed more convicting than the last.

And so, in the summer of 2013, my fearless husband started by hand digging a well on our new parcel of no-mans land. Soon, leaves fell. Then snow. And then he started building, with a single loyal friend, through the most bitterly cold, record-breaking snowy winter on record. They worked at night, after long days in court, using a garage sale generator for power, and built a 1,000-square-foot, off-grid cabin that was finished in spring 2015. Now, six months later, we are about to start on our permanent home at the same 30-acre site. It's a blessing that our property has water, we have improved food storage, seed banks, precious metals, security, books, board games, little comforts.

Yet, we fret because there is always so much more we must do. We still feel woefully unprepared for the many scenarios that seem ripe to implode. We are grateful that we will be able to at least get started and can help a few others along the way. Are we completely comfortable with the reality we are anticipating, no way. Do we sleep better at night because of the scattered efforts we've managed while still living in mainstream America? Yes. And if our greatest wish comes true and nothing happens, we will simply be grateful for the extra sleep that comes with being prepared for anything.

S.M.

"Live like this" became our mantra in 2012. Our family's journey from ignorance towards resilience required redefining our narrative, escaping professional 'success' and the chains of servitude required to achieve it. We sought to improve the quality of our life as much as defend against humanity's risky and deteriorating condition.

With solid consulting skills, both my wife and I found single-issue stories of doom laughably narrow. The three Es and the solid analytics in *The Crash Course* finally helped us conceptualize the dimensions we needed to cover in building a comprehensive action plan.

A few years earlier the economic crises passed our house mostly unnoticed, except that it finally cleared our position on a 10-year waitlist to moor our sailboat on an idyllic island four hours from the city. The air was noticeably clearer there. We knew it would be a good place to recreate, and had aspired to retire to one of the beautiful waterfront homes.

We made weekly trips and stayed over on the boat to clear our heads. By May, our action plan had us trading our whopper mortgage and most of our life savings for free and clear ownership of a neglected plot on the interior of the island. It had enough land for a substantial garden and incoming geese landing on the pond during our house-hunt pretty much clinched the deal.

My wife steered us away from the gloomiest 'prepper instantaneous disaster' scenarios and focused on building the eight forms of capital critical to "living like this." We found our rural neighbors were a godsend. We hadn't even met four of our neighbors in the city. Rural and small town life, in fact any self-sufficiency at all was new to us. Investments in community paid off. We built skills, streamlined our life, and substituted our ingenuity and labor for hired out work.

We found a new love for fewer, simpler, high-quality items built to last and increasingly less processed inputs. We bought wheat in sacks, ground it into our own homemade bread, and found it wonderful. We could at least theoretically grow the wheat ourselves. We graduated from the tyranny of "$5 suspicious-ingredient bread from the store" into the wafting aromas and satisfying production of our own $0.30-a-loaf freshly baked bread. Live like this indeed.

The soil destroying, noisy vibrating 'always in the shop or jammed with a rock, gas-powered rototiller' became a sturdy, silent, and rarely jammed, soil building broad fork. Instead of mechanic and oil dependency, a broad fork is both health dependent and health creating. It seems to fit the virtuous circle of our "live like this" mantra, and the nutrient dense food we grew fueled our aging bodies with surprising amounts of new health and vigor. We vote with our money, broad forks and homemade bread win.

We realized through our study of permaculture that we had just "stacked functions" and have now set about doing lots more of that sort of thing. We still have a ways to go, but feel the chains to the old narrative are broken. We are now free to live like this.

NEXT STEPS &
MORE RESOURCES

Now that you've finished reading this book, it's time to get busy putting its advice into action and building up resilience across all 8 Forms of Capital.

USE THE WORKBOOK

We offer step-by-step guidance on how to do this—including recommendations of specific products and services that Chris, Adam and the PeakProsperity.com community have actually used to good outcome—in *Prosper!*'s companion publication: the *What Should I Do?* Workbook. This workbook is available online at: http://www.peakprosperity.com/WSID

This guide is a living document and will be regularly updated when we have new or improved recommendations to offer.

MORE RESOURCES

Below are additional resources some offered by us, some by others—that we find ourselves directing people to frequently when it comes to resilience-building:

- **PeakProsperity.com Groups** – these free online discussion forums allow you to learn from and collaborate with other like-minded people. *Interest groups* connect you with seasoned experts on specific topics (for example gardening, energy efficiency, and personal and home defense) who are happy to share their knowledge with you. *Local groups* put you in touch with people living in your geographic area, with whom you can collaborate with on a project or social basis. www.peakprosperity.com/groups

- **PeakProsperity.com Enrollment** – those looking to stay on top of the macro developments in real-time can subscribe to our premium analysis. You'll receive full access to our reports, as well as alerts we may issue to warn of impending risks.
www.peakprosperity.com/enroll

- **Endorsed Financial Advisers** – if you're looking for a financial adviser who understands the Three Es, is cautious of today's market risks, and places a high priority on risk management, you can request a free consultation with one we endorse here:
www.greylockpeak.com

- **Buying Gold and Silver** – for those looking for guidance on how best to own precious metals (e.g., physical bullion, stored metal, ETFs, mining stocks) and finding reputable dealers from whom to buy.
http://www.peakprosperity.com/where-to-buy-gold-and-silver

- **Seminars** – looking to dive more deeply into the issues and opportunities raised within this book? Or perhaps hoping to spend time with people as engaged with this material as you are? Come to one of our weekend seminars or a speaking event that's happening near you. You can find the schedule here:
http://www.peakprosperity.com/events

- **Personal Consultations** – have a live conversation with Chris and/ or Adam to address the biggest questions you're grappling with as you work on your resilience plan.
www.peakprosperity.com/consulting

- **Permaculture Consulting** – for those interested in using the natural systems on their property to the fullest extent. This is a permaculture design expert (and Peak Prosperity community member) we recommend highly, who does both on-site and remote consulting work. Mention this book when you contact him to receive a discount:
www.foodproduction101.com/consulting

- **Owning Farmland** – owning farmland is very desirable for many of our community members but, frankly, it's not easy to invest in. Most people either can't afford to buy a farm or aren't interested in operating one. This fund is a popular alternative: it purchases conventionally-farmed land and then "heals" it using sustainable farming practices. Once the soil is declared organic, it sells a variety of produce and

livestock. *At this time, this opportunity is only available to accredited investors.* More can be learned here:
www.peakprosperity.com/farmlandlp

If you find you have questions this book, its companion workbook, the PeakProsperity.com website or the resources listed above can't address, please email us at support@peakprosperity.com and we'll do our best to answer them for you.

EPILOGUE

You are one of the lucky ones.

We know it may not seem that way—having to confront the fearsome state of the world with all of its problems, predicaments and the insanely uncertain decisions that have to be made by each of us in the face of all that. But it's true: *You are one of the lucky ones.*

Those who cannot, will not, or do not see the changes coming will most likely suffer for their blindness. Not because they're any less capable than we are, but they'll be unprepared. And the shocks will be sudden.

It's like the difference between falling off a cliff and taking a gentle, winding path to the bottom. Both get you to the same place, but one is far more perilous.

To adapt gracefully to a world of less stuff, but more meaning, takes time. Acquiring the skills and resources necessary to buffer yourself from the various and sundry potential future shocks takes time and focus. Building social relationships as well as emotional and spiritual capital also takes time. And it's far easier to accomplish all this when times are relatively good and social stress is relatively low, as life is today.

Because you are considering undertaking these steps now, while the world is still relatively calm, means that you have the opportunity to prosper. Not just in some possible future of disruption. But here, now. Today.

In many ways, this book and our life's work is really just a call to assume more responsibility for ourselves. Or perhaps we should say *resume* taking responsibility for ourselves, because none of the recommendations we've written in this book would sound novel to your great-grandparents.

Know how to do some useful things, keep a deep pantry, know your neighbors, and help when you can.

While those were golden rules once-upon-a-time, today we face greater challenges as nations and as a species than ever before. The magnitude of the problems we face is daunting. Frightening, even. But there's nothing more or less required of you than to become the change you wish to see.

The very *worst* that could happen if you devote time, money and effort towards expanding your depth in each of the 8 Forms of Capital is that you will be healthier, have more true wealth, be more at peace, be less stressed, have deeper more fulfilling relationships, and be surrounded by living beauty. Even if we're entirely wrong about how the future unfolds, everything in here is still worth doing.

However, should one of the more desperate future scenarios unfold, then your dedication to building resilience today will be the best investment you have ever made. You'll be far less vulnerable to crisis, able to help others who aren't, and much better positioned to take advantage of all the new opportunities that will eventually follow.

It's our sincere hope that you've read this book carefully and taken its advice to heart. We truly care about reaching as many people as we can, but especially you—one of those with open eyes, ears and a big heart.

This book is intended to be a living document because our learning about these topics is both fluid and continuous. New fascinating research shapes our understanding of what it means to be human and how our DNA blueprint instructs us. Better ideas come along almost daily and new solutions, too. So we invite you to visit PeakProsperity.com to engage with us and the Peak Prosperity community in following all of the exciting and, frankly, sometimes troubling developments that happen every day. There we analyze, debate and discuss: *How do the latest insights impact our forecasts for the future?* There you'll find like-minded thinkers, tips, guidance, and helpful advice as you—together with us—navigate one of the most exciting times to be alive.

Thank you for reading this book and for joining us in our quest to create a world worth inheriting. May the next steps you take from here place you on the path to a future of security, happiness, and abundance.

In short, we have one great wish for you: to *Prosper!*

WEB LINKS

$\mathbf{H}$ere are the web linking URLs for each of the podcast and article callouts made throughout this book:

1. Energy-related chapters (19-22) from The Crash Course video series
   www.peakprosperity.com/crashcourse

2. Exponential Growth chapter from The Crash Course video series
   www.peakprosperity.com/video/85828/playlist/92161/crash-course-chapter-3-exponential-growth

3. Economy-related chapters (6-18) from The Crash Course video series
   www.peakprosperity.com/crashcourse

4. Dan Ariely podcast on behavioral economics
   www.peakprosperity.com/blog/dan-ariely-decodes-why-humans-are-hard-wired-inflate/50338

5. *How to Hedge Against A Market Correction* article
   www.peakprosperity.com/insider/87196/how-hedge-against-market-correction (premium subscription required)

6. Philip Haslam podcast on Zimbabwe's currency collapse
   www.peakprosperity.com/podcast/92151/philip-haslam-when-money-destroys-nations

7. Woody Tasch podcast on the Slow Money movement
   www.peakprosperity.com/podcast/87494/woody-tasch-slow-money

8. Craig Wichner podcast on investing in farmland
www.peakprosperity.com/podcast/86565/new-opportunity-
investing-productive-farmland

9. Singing Frogs Farm podcast on soil management
www.peakprosperity.com/podcast/92727/paul-elizabeth-kaiser-
sustainable-farming-20

10. Chris's personal health & fitness transformation article
www.peakprosperity.com/blog/getting-shape-new-me/62871

11. Adam's personal health & fitness transformation article
www.peakprosperity.com/blog/92302/new-me-round-2

12. Mark Sisson podcast on fitness
www.peakprosperity.com/podcast/80763/mark-sisson-2-2-2013

13. Robb Wolf podcast on nutrition
www.peakprosperity.com/podcast/83424/robb-wolf-science-
behind-healthy-diet-fitness

14. Chris Kresser podcast on functional health
www.peakprosperity.com/podcast/87723/chris-kresser-
functional-health

15. Toby Hemenway podcast on permaculture
www.peakprosperity.com/podcast/85511/toby-hemenway-
explaining-permaculture

16. PeakProsperity.com's Agriculture/Permaculture Group
www.peakprosperity.com/group/agriculture-permaculture

17. PeakProsperity.com's Online Groups home page
www.peakprosperity.com/groups

18. Mormon food storage article
www.peakprosperity.com/blog/food-storage-dummies/55478

19. Community food storage day article
www.peakprosperity.com/forum/successful-food-
storage-day-9-familes-4-tons-5-hours-lessons-learned-
recommendations/27519

20. NASA podcast on coronal mass ejection risks
www.peakprosperity.com/podcast/82542/nasa-our-technology-
dependent-lifestyle-vulnerable-solar-flares

21. EMP Task Force podcast on EMP risks
www.peakprosperity.com/podcast/92943/former-cia-director-
were-not-doing-nearly-enough-protect-against-emp-threat

22. PeakProsperity.com's guide to Emotional Resilience
www.peakprosperity.com/wiki/193/emotional-resiliency

23. FERFal podcast on Argentina's currency collapse
www.peakprosperity.com/podcast/84705/ferfal-heres-what-
looks-when-your-countrys-economy-collapses

24. PeakProsperity.com's guide to Building Community
www.peakprosperity.com/blog/building-community/47502

25. James Rawles podcast on relocation
www.peakprosperity.com/podcast/83076/james-wesley-rawles-
homesteading-relocation-resilience

About the Authors

CHRIS MARTENSON, PhD

Chris Martenson, PhD (Duke), MBA (Cornell) is an economic researcher and futurist specializing in energy and resource depletion, and co-founder of PeakProsperity.com (along with Adam Taggart). As one of the early econobloggers who forecasted the housing market collapse and stock market correction years in advance, Chris rose to prominence with the launch of his seminal video seminar: *The Crash Course* which has also been published in book form (Wiley, March 2011). It's a popular and extremely well-regarded distillation of the interconnected forces in the Economy, Energy and the Environment (the "Three Es" as Chris calls them) that are shaping the future, one that will be defined by increasing challenges to growth as we have known it.

In addition to the analysis and commentary he writes for his site PeakProsperity.com, Chris' insights are in high demand by the media as well as academic, civic, and private organizations around the world, including institutions such as the UN, the UK House of Commons and US State Legislatures.

PeakProsperity.com